WHY CAPITALISM?

WHY CAPITALISM?

ALLAN H. MELTZER

OXFORD
UNIVERSITY PRESS

OXFORD
UNIVERSITY PRESS

Oxford University Press, Inc., publishes works that further
Oxford University's objective of excellence
in research, scholarship, and education.

Oxford   New York
Auckland   Cape Town   Dar es Salaam   Hong Kong   Karachi
Kuala Lumpur   Madrid   Melbourne   Mexico City   Nairobi
New Delhi   Shanghai   Taipei   Toronto

With offices in
Argentina   Austria   Brazil   Chile   Czech Republic   France   Greece
Guatemala   Hungary   Italy   Japan   Poland   Portugal   Singapore
South Korea   Switzerland   Thailand   Turkey   Ukraine   Vietnam

Published by Oxford University Press, Inc.
198 Madison Avenue, New York, New York 10016

www.oup.com

Oxford is a registered trademark of Oxford University Press

Library of Congress Cataloging-in-Publication Data
Meltzer, Allan H.
Why capitalism? / Allan H. Meltzer.
    p.   cm.
Includes bibliographical references and index.
ISBN 978-0-19-985957-3 (cloth : alk. paper) 1. Capitalism. I. Title.
HB501.M45   2012
330.12'2—dc23   2011020507

9 8 7 6 5 4 3 2 1

Printed in the United States of America
on acid-free paper

I dedicate this book to my grandchildren hoping that they will come to share my passion for liberty.

CONTENTS

PREFACE

It was with a mixture of surprise and disbelief in the fall of 2008 that I read journalists' commentaries on the end of capitalism. Many welcomed the expansion of regulation and government intervention and the weakening of market competition as a regulator. Several journalists asked me to comment on the alleged end of capitalism. Did they not see that capitalism had become the dominant form of economic organization that had spread in the past 50 years from a few countries in North America and Western Europe to Asia, Latin America, and now to Africa? I often wonder if they are pleased by the increase in regulation that coincides with sluggish growth and persistent high unemployment.

This book offers my explanation of the success of democratic capitalism and the failure of alternatives. Democratic capitalism has three unequaled strengths. It is the only system that achieves both economic growth and individual freedom, and it adapts to the many diverse cultures in the world. Adapting to cultures means that it works well with people as they are, not as someone would like to make them. Democracy works to remove the most common criticism of capitalism—that it generates inequality in income distribution. Voters choose the tax rates and income redistribution that satisfies a majority of voters, never all of them.

Alternatives to capitalism, whether socialism, communism, fascism, or some religious orthodoxies, offer some group's utopian vision of mankind that becomes the one "right path." Utopian visions and orthodoxies always bring enforcement, often brutal enforcement. The 20th century saw many such outcomes. None achieved both higher living standards and greater individual freedom. National Socialism, Soviet and Chinese Communism instead produced mass murders of millions. This should have extinguished the appeal of utopian visions, but it has not. Many still believe that social justice can only be achieved by ending or severely regulating capitalism. These essays dispute that notion.

Long ago John Locke recognized that collective action is the efficient response to some social problems. Voters in democratic capitalist countries can vote to redistribute and regulate. Regulation restricts competitive solutions, but regulation often fails to achieve efficient or desirable outcomes because it is subject to capture by the regulated and to circumvention by those most affected. Regulation works best when it changes the incentives of the regulated. Much regulation, instead, creates incentives for circumvention and corruption.

Capitalism is not a perfect solution to human problems. Perfect solutions are utopian; capitalism is a human institution that works with humans as they are. I share the view strongly taken by early Christianity that Immanuel Kant expressed very well. People are not perfect; capitalism and all its many alternatives are not responsible for what goes wrong.

People, most often people in powerful positions, are. Capitalism disperses and limits power while the alternatives concentrate power in a few hands.

The chapters that follow show the influence of Immanuel Kant, Karl Popper, Friedrich Hayek, Milton Friedman, and my former teachers and friends Karl Brunner and Armen Alchian. The path that I follow combines what I received from them, together with some that I added during a lifetime of teaching, learning, and writing scholarly publications. Work with my friend and former colleague Scott Richard has a prominent place in the development of ideas about democratic capitalism. I also owe a debt to the MBA students at Carnegie Mellon's Tepper School, who for many years have elected my course on capitalism and commented on the materials, and to Lynn Chu, who read and edited the manuscript to make it more readable.

I have spent more than 50 years as a teacher and scholar, so I have accumulated many debts. My thanks to the many colleagues and friends who helped and encouraged me. Most of all, I am indebted to my wife, Marilyn, for her unflagging support and encouragement. Special thanks also to Richard Scaife and the Scaife Foundations and the Bradley Foundation for many years of support. My assistant, Alberta Ragan, has prepared my manuscripts and assisted ably in many projects with grace and excellence for more than 30 years. Thank you.

Pittsburgh, May 2011

WHY CAPITALISM?

WHY CAPITALISM?

OPPONENTS OF CAPITALISM and free markets frequently claim that one or another of the periodic crises that occur foreshadow the end of capitalism. Most recently, such predictions followed the recent financial crisis. The 2008 housing-credit crisis was a serious, but temporary, decline—not a permanent loss of wealth, much less "the end of capitalism," as some proclaimed at the time. Capitalist systems have weathered many more serious problems and all survived this one.

Today, capitalism is the economic system that guides most of the world—having overcome unremitting intellectual hostility, as well as military hostility from Communist nations during the Cold War. Yet even China and formerly socialist India have embraced market economies. Both recently pledged to maintain them, along with South Korea and Australia.

Capitalist systems are not rigid, nor are they all the same. Capitalism is unique in permitting change and adaptation, so different societies tend to develop different rules and processes, often reflecting cultural requirements. What all share is ownership of the means of production by individuals who remain relatively free to choose their activities, where they work, what they buy and sell, and at what prices. As an institution for producing goods and services, capitalism's success rests on a foundation of a rule of law, which protects individual rights to property, and, in the first instance, aligns rewards to values produced. Working hand in hand with the rule of law, capitalism gives its participants incentives to act as society desires, typically rewarding hard work, intelligence, persistence, and innovation. If too many laws work against this, capitalism may suffer disruptions. Capitalism embraces competition. Competition rewards those who build value, and offers buyers choices and competitive prices. Like any system, capitalism has successes and failures—but it is the only system known to humanity that increases both growth and freedom.

Critics of capitalism often complain that the distribution of income generated by the market system is unequal. They point to capitalism's frequent periods of unemployment and instability, and its rewards for selfish rather than for socially beneficial, cooperative activity. Some favor heavy regulation to achieve social goals. Others favor putting a public institution, or the state, in control of allocating resources. Talk of equity and fairness generally means wealth redistribution. But no economic system focused on property confiscation and redistribution has ever sustained both growth and personal freedom.

Critics of capitalism usually ignore or discount incentives, which are part of the engine that drives progress. Income differences reflect differences in individual ability and the value that markets place on particular activities at particular times. The relation of reward to effort or achievement may not be precise, but it is positive.

Many defenders of capitalism present it as a moral system—that it is morally right for people to use their own resources as they choose. The problem with the moral defense of capitalism is that it ignores or discounts the occurrence of venal or illegal activity and expedient, self-serving decisions.

All people are not honest all of the time. Greed leads people astray. Generally accepted moral principles also don't make specific decisions any easier for a society to agree upon. People who share common moral principles often disagree about their precise application—the death penalty and abortion are among many ever-present examples.

It is of course true that any system works best if the participants share moral principles such as honesty and commitment. Moral principles are important in any economic system. Yet these are not part of the system; they are attributes of individuals. Capitalism and its incentives may be a more potent force encouraging honest dealing, if only because competition induces honest behavior more often than other systems. But capitalism works in corrupt environments as well.

The rule of law is the principal, partial substitute for a moral code. To function efficiently, or to function at all, a capitalist system requires rules, many of which impose moral principles. The law must protect individuals and property, enforce contracts, sustain faith in the stability of the system over time, reduce uncertainty, and respond to political and social pressures.

Long ago, the great German philosopher Immanuel Kant told us why the moral defense of capitalism couldn't be relied upon. In 1784, he wrote that "out of timber so crooked as that from which man is made, nothing entirely straight can be carved." Everyone is not honest, a point reinforced by periodic scandals. Kant's statement restates medieval Christian orthodoxy. Humans are morally imperfect, and so are their institutions.

Private and public officials often break the law. Kant's dictum applies at least as much to public as to private officials, and criminality cannot be reduced by choosing socialism or the welfare state. More likely, it is increased: Siemens was convicted of bribing officials in many countries; Enron, WorldCom, and Madoff are recent examples of unethical and illegal corporate behavior; Watergate and the Russian takeover of oil companies are examples of public malfeasance; bribery and corruption of officials are recurring problems in China. There are simply too many examples to cite. Capitalism and markets disperse power; centralization and collective action concentrates power and increases the cost that the public bears.

Capitalism survives and spreads because it recognizes Kant's principle. People differ: some give bibles, but some sell pornography. Unlike its alternatives, capitalism does not take a utopian view of economic organization or replace man's choices with a legal command that someone's idea of perfection be implemented. It permits a choice for change, then allows change to be rejected after one sees the outcome. It recognizes that all change is not necessarily an improvement and will not necessarily be welcomed by all, and it accommodates those differences by letting individuals choose for themselves. Over time, people observe others' successes and follow suit. Capitalism therefore has a means of removing failures. Competition eliminates less efficient activities and strengthens survivors by encouraging them to adapt to change.

Socialism and other utopian systems are more rigid. They represent someone's belief in the aims of a stated ideal that certain "good people" embrace—if movies are too violent, then they must change; if television is too banal, it must be improved. But such change is always an imposed choice by some individual and on lines subject to uncertain or disputable interpretations. Freedom lets people make their own choices, even if they violate someone else's idea of proper norms or right conduct. Socialism seeks to restrict choices only to those that officials will permit. Capitalism accepts that in a market economy some people's choices won't please everyone, for individual tastes and desires differ. Like Kant, capitalism does not seek utopia but lets markets accommodate differences, leaving most decisions to individuals, who then can learn from the outcomes of their own choices and by observing the outcomes of their neighbors' choices.

Freedom of choice brings more satisfaction to more people—even in nonmarket situations. Nothing assures that taken together everyone's choices will meet any particular ideal of the good, the wholesome, or the moral—yet choice in a capitalist system will nevertheless, at the individual level, satisfy many by continuing to satisfy their changing demands. Further, the choices individuals make inform others, thus enabling the market to respond to demand.

Competition brings choice and improved relevance not only to commerce but also to religion. James Madison believed that competing churches would prove stronger than an established state church—because each would appeal to its members and try to attract others. Time proved Madison right. In Europe, the state supports established churches, yet organized religion is weak; the public rejects the state's religion monopoly by simply not participating. Human intelligence is found everywhere, yet the United States has the world's strongest, most progressive universities because its universities compete for the best and brightest of scholars and students, and for money; our competitive impulse drives change, ideas, and innovation. Because U.S. universities attract quality students and researchers from all over the world, they remain vibrant and exciting places operating at the frontier of knowledge.

Capitalism does not solve all problems efficiently. Long ago, John Locke recognized that some services call for collective action. For instance, society was clearly better off if everyone paid taxes to support a public service such as police or night watchmen. Locke ruled out a complete system of market allocation without any public intervention but created the rationale for collective action in place of individual choice for some types of activity, called public goods.

Once we accept that collective action is the preferred method of allocating some resources, we introduce a government with the power to tax, and the system becomes a mixed capitalist system.

Revealingly, the recent outcry over the financial crisis blamed unregulated markets and deregulation as a cause of the financial crisis. Without doubt bankers made mistakes that proved costly to everyone. Inept regulation is more to blame. All financial markets have been heavily regulated for decades. After 1999—when investment banks and commercial banks were permitted to merge with the removal of the 1933 prohibition imposed by the Glass-Steagall Act—very little deregulation occurred. No other country adopted similar regulations. No one has yet explained how ending the separation between these businesses, formerly required by Glass-Steagall, contributed to the crisis. The Basel Agreement required banks to hold more reserves if they increased risk. Regulation thus addressed the problem but was overlooked or disregarded. The banks responded to Basel regulation with evasion by putting their risky assets in off-balance sheet entities. So in effect, Basel increased risk by inspiring evasion that was nontransparent. Simultaneously, investors were overassured that regulatory oversight existed and could be confidently relied upon, when it could not be. This followed my first law of regulation. Lawyers and bureaucrats regulate. Markets circumvent regulation. My second law of regulations says: Regulations are static. Markets are dynamic. If circumvention does not occur at first, it will occur later. Regulation then often misleads the innocent.

Effective regulation rewards intelligent transactions and punishes bad ones. Regulation may create a monopoly, raise barriers to entry, or incentivize socially desirable behavior. For example, to limit banks' size and appetite for risk, regulation might require that capital increase faster than assets. Increasing firm size increases costs that managers and stockholders, not the public, should pay for.

In any mixed system, the distribution of responsibility and authority between public and private sectors has to be governed by rules. Most capitalist countries run public goods such as national defense and the police democratically, with voters choosing how much to be taxed versus the size of government. Voters decide matters at a high level of abstraction, leaving government to set precise rules for market behavior. Democracy means that majorities can shift responsibility from the individual to a collective—that is, to the creation of a welfare state.

DEMOCRATIC CAPITALISM

Voters can also act to collectively provide public goods other than defense and police protection by, for example, blurring the lines between private and public authorities and responsibilities, increasing or reducing the government's role in redistributing income, and regulating private sector activities. Elections often are about choosing between the party that favors economic growth through lower tax rates and less government regulation versus the party that wants more government programs to redistribute income and expand government's role and size, thereby supplanting private goods or extending activities in place already, such as education, health care, or nursery schools. Government programs can provide services at below market prices by shifting the cost of their operations to other taxpayers, current and future. A desire to expand access to such services does not necessarily mean that they must be supplied by the government.

Democratic capitalism allows voters sometimes to favor higher growth and at other times to favor redistribution. Critics of capitalism who emphasize "fairness" often do not recognize that this word is hard to define, for the system is not static, but ever-changing, with the "fair" result changing with it. The word "fairness" is often a way of avoiding mention of the real goal of such critics, redistribution. Proponents of fairness generally want more private goods to be supplied publicly at subsidized prices or increased spending on welfare—to be paid for by taxes on those with above median income or by the issuance of debt to be paid by later generations. Much legislation or regulation presented as "fair" leaves large debts to future generations.

Democratic capitalism tends to deal with the Kantian problem by cracking down on excesses by owners or managers of capital assets with regulations that seek to deter socially undesirable behaviors or to tax behaviors or outcomes that majorities dislike. Recent attacks on smoking show how changes in public attitudes drive legislation. Because outlawing alcohol and narcotics were famously unsuccessful in the past, today's anti-smoking crusades seem to be restricted to raising taxes on tobacco sales rather than a ban.

Regulation to achieve social objectives has two major problems. The first law of regulation says that lawyers and bureaucrats develop regulations, but markets learn how to circumvent those that cost them money. The second says that the results of regulation often differ from the regulation's goal or plan.

Circumvention occurs in many regulated markets. The Basel agreement meant to regulate but wound up increasing risk. Similarly, the goal of campaign finance reform to rid politics of the noxious influence of money and to cap presidential candidate spending to a sum regulators would decide at first appeared laudable. But it failed: the 2008 presidential election turned out to be more costly than ever, with only one of the major party candidates accepting taxpayer funds and a limit on spending. The legislation limited spending by candidates and parties but not by interest groups. The result was to further weaken political parties, which work to harmonize divergent interests, and increase the influence of single-issue groups, which often work to magnify differences and so make policy compromise more difficult. This was not the outcome proponents of McCain-Feingold or similar campaign spending legislation had promised or anticipated. Quite the opposite.

Regulation is socially useful if it aligns private and social costs, as when people pool funds for the "night watchman"; collective action might be more efficient (less costly) than private. But not all regulations meet that test. If I were to articulate a third law of regulation, it would be that the aim of regulation in a market economy should be to equate private and social costs because whenever it doesn't, the regulation simply invites circumvention. Then, although the regulation gives the appearance of protection, the world may in fact have only been made riskier by lowering individuals' guard against caveat emptor. Many inefficient regulations stay in place indefinitely because they benefit a special interest group who then makes it their business to sustain them. Agricultural subsidies for high-income farmers, for instance, are programs that persist and even grow. Peltzman (2004) offers another reason: the "capture" of regulatory agencies by the regulated, a phenomenon now supported by a large economic literature. Under democratic capitalism, costly distortions of this kind seem unavoidable.

Many critics of deregulation cite the Gramm, Leach, Bliley Act, which repealed the separation of commercial and investment banking established under the Glass-Steagall Act of 1933. Such critics usually don't specify what problems this repeal caused or recognize that Glass-Steagall had been circumvented long before its repeal. Investment banks and commercial banks engaged in similar activities. The main remaining difference was that commercial banks held demand deposits. Like investment banks, they financed many of their activities in the overnight market. Costly regulation encourages circumvention. Compliance with regulation is bought from legislators by granting the regulated industry a monopoly or by enacting strong penalties against circumvention. This suggests that more research on the political economy of regulation, its persistence, and its evasion—and what types of regulation are most efficient in what circumstances—is needed.

Democratic capitalism alternates between more and less intrusive government, based on overall voter preference for more or less redistribution, or higher or slower growth, usually based on just past results. Periods of low growth make voters favor reducing taxes and regulation. Periods of sustained growth often spread the distribution of income, causing voters to prefer larger transfers and higher current or future tax rates (Meltzer and Richard, 1981).

Raising tax rates or regulation shifts control of resource allocation from private to public managers. This does not avoid the Kantian problem; the form may change, but humanity's problems remain, as neither the public nor the private sector contains only virtuous people. The many examples of corruption, bribery, and misfeasance cited above are a just a small sample. Offenses such as bribery can be either public or private and are common in many nations, but they are most common where government officials have the most authority.

Reduction of air pollution is a public good. Everyone can pollute by adding noxious gasses to the air. Economists would have users pay by taxing carbon. Higher gasoline taxes stimulate production of less harmful substitutes and the search for alternatives. Many voters do not want to pay an additional tax, so politicians are unwilling to vote for such taxes. The alternative is regulation, which is less efficient, but the costs paid are less observable and their burden can seem to be imposed on producers, who then are blamed for shifting the cost to consumers.

Public sector regulators are inclined to be more cautious and more anxious to avoid failure than entrepreneurial capitalists. Decades ago Sam Peltzman showed that the Federal Drug Administration placed too much weight on avoiding drugs and medications with potentially harmful side effects that were relatively minor because they failed to account for the losses from restricting the benefits of such drugs, a bias that has never been corrected. This outcome is very different from the choices people would make in the marketplace. And, like all regulation, rule making and rule enforcement can be pressured or controlled by special interest groups.

Regulatory "capture" by interest groups occurs often. The Federal Reserve often acts as guardian of the New York banks' interests. The Federal Aviation Administration discourages and even punishes employees who call for strict enforcement of safety rules. There are many other examples of misdirected government regulation.

Well-run companies plan for the long term. But governments typically follow the political cycle, a much shorter term. Private sector companies make investments that increase employment, productivity, and output. Public spending responds to public pressures for redistribution. For example, AIDS research receives substantial funding because its advocates are active; other diseases such as Alzheimer's for which organized advocacy is lacking receive less. Although much spending is defended or promoted as a way to help the neediest, large spending programs transfer mostly to the middle class, as that is where most of the voters are.

Democracy is another way to allocate resources. Generally, those who succeed in the marketplace favor allocation by markets, not governments. Those who do not succeed favor government redistribution, joined by those who dislike capitalism or prefer collectively mandated "social justice" over market efficiency. Actual social outcomes are a compromise between the two aims.

Congress very often approves legislation but leaves detailed regulation to the regulators. This substitutes the rule of regulations for the rule of law, thereby reducing the extent to which we have a government of laws, not a government of men (or women). Reducing the scope of the rule of law damages capitalism. Examples abound. Sarbanes-Oxley legislation reduced the attractiveness of U.S. equity markets. Many foreign firms left. Much regulation has the effect of replacing the rule of law with arbitrary decisions by lawyers and bureaucrats.

ALTERNATIVES TO CAPITALISM

The critics of capitalism always decry "greed" and "self-interest" and invoke "social justice" and "fairness." Socialism, Communism, or authoritarianism are generally proposed as an alternative, yet these systems have persisted mainly under police states. This is not accidental. Orthodoxy must be enforced on the unwilling. The main alternative is the regulated welfare state, which is discussed in the next chapter.

Anti-capitalists err in three ways: first, by ignoring Kant's warning about human imperfection; second, by ignoring individual differences while substituting in the name of proclaimed goals such as equality, fairness, or justice rigid direction in place of individual choice. Justice and fairness are imprecise terms subject to individual interpretations with no fixed standard. Their third error comes in practice: the choices of the ruler often have to be enforced using fear, terror, prison, or punishment. The 20th century is rife with promised ends that were never realized that turned into a justification for deplorable means.

Assigning decision-making authority over resource allocation does not eliminate crime, greed, self-dealing, conflict of interest, or corruption. Experience tells us these problems remain, regardless of the system's form. Ludwig von Mises recognized in the 1920s that top-down price fixing and resource allocation eliminated important information from the system. Capitalism allocates by letting relative prices adjust around the trade-offs expressed by buyers' individually expressed needs, which constitute their overall demand. Replacing consumer choices with an official decision fails to incorporate these accurate, individual, cumulative buy-sell data into the system, thus distorting prices. At the set price, some will gain, but others will lose. By contrast, a freer system allows market equilibrium prices to evolve based on the actual, accurate demands of all. Those who lose in the ordered system would have preferred to choose for themselves.

Not all socialist societies have turned brutal. In the 19th century, followers of Robert Owen, the Amana people, and many others chose a socialist system. Israeli pioneers chose a collectivist system, the kibbutz. Still, none of these arrangements produced sustainable growth, and none survived. All faced the problem of imposing allocative decisions that satisfied the decision-making group and sometimes reflected a majority view but often did not. Capitalism recognizes that where individual wants differ, the market should be free to respond, so that minorities can develop their own best outcome. Walk down the aisles of a modern supermarket. There are products that satisfy many different tastes or beliefs. Diversity of this degree does not occur in nonmarket economies.

Theodor Adorno was a leading critic of postwar capitalism who found popular culture vulgar, as it developed in his native Germany and the West. He distrusted workers' choices and called for a socialism that would uphold intellectual values. Capitalism, he said, valued work too highly and true leisure too little. He disliked jazz, so when Hitler banned it in the 1930s, he didn't object. But Adorno proposed no way of achieving the culture he preferred except to legislate his tastes and ban all the choices he disliked. This appealed to people who shared his view. But many preferred American pop culture, whenever they had the right to choose.

Capitalism permits choices and the freedom to make them. Some radio stations play jazz, some offer opera and symphonies, others play pop music. Advertisers choose what radio or television shows to sponsor. Under socialism, the public watches and hears what someone else chooses for them and are allowed little individual choice.

The Templeton Foundation recently publicized various responses prominent intellectuals gave to the question: "Does the free market corrode moral character?" Several noted that free markets require a legal and political framework and the rule of law. One blot upon the morality of law by democratic choice is the legality, up to the 19th century, of slavery. Public opinion, a bloody war, and, finally, the law eventually removed that stain, and still another century would elapse before the law forbade race discrimination.

Most respondents took a mixed stand. The philosopher John Gray admitted that greed and envy were driving forces under capitalism but also produced growth and raised living standards, thus benefitting many. Greed also produces Enrons and WorldComs, but it is less a characteristic of a system than a vice of individuals, and it is at least as prevalent under socialism. Michael Walzer thought political activity also corrodes moral character but claimed that political activity was regulated more effectively. Another respondent thought the question had to be weighed relative to other social systems, and Bernard-Henri Levy asserted that alternatives to capitalism such as fascism and communism were far worse.

None mentioned Kant's view of mankind as consisting of a range of individuals of varying moral character. Institutional social arrangements such as democracy and capitalism appear to correlate with more morality in that no democratic capitalist country has produced crimes of a scale comparable to the mass murders committed by Hitler's Germany, Mao's China, or Lenin and Stalin's Soviet Union.

As Lord Acton warned, power corrupts. Some use power to impose their will, while proclaiming that noble ends justify the use of force or even tyranny to control the opposition. Communism proclaimed a vision of equality of outcome that it never came close to attaining. Individuals differ about what is good for themselves, so that a particular type of equality is difficult if not impossible to achieve without considerable dissatisfaction. After every national election, the dissatisfied voters include both those who wanted more redistribution and higher tax rates and those who wanted the opposite.

Kant's principle warns that utopian visions are unattainable. Capitalism does not offer a static vision of perfection and harmony. Democratic capitalism combines freedom, opportunity, growth, progress, and competition with restrictions on less desirable behavior. It creates societies that treat men and women as they are, not as in some utopian vision. In *The Open Society and Its Enemies* (1945), Karl Popper showed why utopian visions become totalitarian—because the state becomes obsessed with preventing all deviations from the utopian ideal.

The Enrons, WorldComs, and so forth show that dishonest individuals rise along with honest individuals. A scandal uncovered or a political promise unfulfilled hardly signifies that capitalism has failed, however, although it is true that after 25 to 40 years of talk, promises, and proposals about energy, education, health care, and cocaine and other drugs, little if any progress is visible on these issues.

In the last years we have seen major errors by government or its agents. For example, the Federal Reserve "rescued" American International Group (AIG) by using billions of taxpayer dollars, yet AIG had three profitable divisions, including a highly successful insurance company. Soon after, the taxpayers paid to keep General Motors and Chrysler from bankruptcy, though bankruptcy court would have been a better outcome for bondholders. Even if the companies repay the advances, the system will suffer because some large firms will take on excessive risk expecting to be spared if losses occur. Last August, the government lost six nuclear warheads (which were later found on B-52 bombers flying over the United States). Congress approved purchases of ethanol made from corn that raised the world price of food but did not reduce pollution. Government promises to pay for old-age pensions and health care far exceed any feasible revenues to pay for those promises, and Congress fails to develop a feasible plan. The estimated present value of the nation's unfunded health care promises is $70 to $80 trillion dollars. No private plan would be allowed to operate this way.

GROWTH AND PROGRESS

After World War II, especially after 1960, the developed countries led by the United States worked to raise growth rates in poor countries of the world. There were two experiments. The former Soviet Union and its fellow Communist countries controlled property and directed resource use according to plans developed by a central bureaucracy. Capitalist countries relied on opening to the international market and resource allocation based on market demand and individual choice.

The historic results are clear. Capitalism and the market system proved much more effective at development and reducing poverty than planning systems either in India, whose government is democratically chosen but previously socialist (many of India's leaders having been taught by socialist professors at the London School of Economics), or in authoritarian regimes such as the Soviet Union or China. There is not a single example of sustained successful growth under traditional Communism. The contrast was clear by the end of the 1980s in the comparison between North and South Korea, East and West Germany, and China compared to the Chinese diasporas of Asia.

Recent research charts national economic growth as a function of 38 observable components in five categories as a proxy for relative freedom versus socialism: size of government, legal structure, access to sound money, openness to trade and exchange, and regulation (Gwartney and Larson, 1996). Gwartney and Larson found that in countries with higher rates of investment, higher productivity growth, more foreign direct investment, and stricter adherence to the rule of law, per capita income rose at a compound rate of 3.44 percent in the freest countries, compared to average growth of 0.37 percent in "not free" countries. Intermediate countries had intermediate growth, 1.67 percent.

The failure of alternatives to capitalism and free markets is shown most strikingly by those systems' abandonment by India, China, and most of the former Communist world, who have seen a sustained, dramatic reduction in poverty after finally joining the world trading system and encouraging private ownership of resources, including capital. Many more people improved their living standards since 1990 than in 50 years of government planned development, regulation, and centrally directed resource allocation. Capitalism and the market have proved far better than the state at reducing poverty and raising living standards. Once this development became clear, perennial critics of capitalism turned to other reasons to oppose it. In her book, Margaret Thatcher (1993, p. 625) described such critics' reaction to her success at reforming the British economy, increasing productivity, and reducing inflation.

> Deprived for the moment at least of the opportunity to chastise the Government and blame free enterprise capitalism for failing to create jobs and raise living standards, the left turned their attention to non-economic issues. The idea that the state was the engine of economic progress was discredited— and even more so as the failures of communism became more widely known. But was the price of capitalist prosperity too high? Was it not resulting in gross and offensive materialism, traffic congestion and pollution? . . .
>
> [W]as not the 'quality of life' being threatened?
>
> I found all this misguided and hypocritical. If socialism had produced economic success the same critics would have been celebrating in the streets.

Socialism as a development model faces several obstacles. One is the reduced ability to recognize mistakes and act on that knowledge. A venture capitalist knows all of his investments won't succeed, so he must decide whether to advance more capital or close the firm. The capitalist facing the loss of his own investment decides based on his estimate of expected future return. The socialist uses different criteria. Admitting error is personally costly and requires layoffs. Faced with uncertainty about future outcomes, the socialist and the capitalist choose different outcomes when faced with a risk of shutting down an enterprise that may become profitable and the risk of supporting a failing enterprise. Workers, voters, lose employment. On average the capitalist, rather than the socialist, is more willing to close. The concentration of successful innovation in capitalist countries suggests that the capitalist strategy produces better results for society, as well as for investors and workers over the long run.

Capitalism rewards innovators, so it encourages innovation from anyone willing to invest in new ideas. Competitive markets drive improvements in product and output. Socialism concentrates decision making in a small group. Fewer new ideas develop. The freedom to fail or to gain that drives innovation, change, and progress is absent from the socialist structure. Capitalism without failure is like religion without sin. It doesn't work well.

Some innovations might be inconsistent with religious or moral standards. Critics of capitalism seize upon these arguments to condemn the choices that capitalism and freedom permit and instead promote their own preferences in place of market-driven choices. Democratic systems don't sustain unpopular rules meant to control the public's choices for very long.

Socialism, or any system based on an orthodoxy or a plan for the promotion of the "good," inevitably begins with persuasion and ends with coercion. Any deviation from orthodoxy is a step away from "the good." Hayek's *Road to Serfdom* (1944) showed why government planning is inconsistent with democratic choice.

The consistent, repeated failure of all types of socialist planning and state ownership of the means of production is now widely recognized. Critics of capitalism and promoters of alternatives now focus on advocating a welfare state, thereby transferring decisions to a bureaucracy. During the prosperous years after World War II, voters in all developed capitalist economies chose to increase redistribution, mainly by regulating, taxing, and spending.

INCOME DISTRIBUTION

The distribution of income is a major policy issue in every democratic capitalist nation's elections. There are fewer rich than poor or middle class. Fifty percent of the votes decide an election. The income of the median voter lies below the mean income, so a majority of voters can redistribute income. Early in the history of the American republic, Alexis de Tocqueville warned about the temptation for the voting majority to tax the incomes of those above the mean. His warning remains relevant. There are many examples of redistributive policy carried out for the benefit of the poor. One problem is that the poor are not the same as the lowest 10 or 20 percent of the statistical income distribution. People can be in the lowest tail temporarily. Also many of the poor do not vote. Older people and middle income people do, and they get more attention from politicians.

Angus Maddison, the leading researcher on the history of economic growth, found that by the year 1000 Asian countries led all others in per capita income. By 1820, the capitalist economies of Western Europe and the United States reached twice the Asian average. By 1950, the difference was wider.

Several Asian countries then adopted capitalist methods and the gap narrowed. After Japan and South Korea demonstrated to Asia that growth was a capitalist, not a Western, force, other nations followed, eventually including China and India.

Critics often complain about the gap in income between highest and lowest income groups. U.S. data show that since 1975, household income at the 90th percentile (in 2003 dollars) rose faster than household income at the 10th highest percentile in every five year period except 1990–95. Relative (real) income of the 90th percentile rose from 10.8 times the 10th percentile to 13.7 times. Comparisons that use median household income are misleading, however, because more households today have only a single person (earner) or a retired single person.

Sweden is often used as a model of humane capitalism. There is no doubt that Sweden tried hard to redistribute income. In 1975 the top 1 percent of consumer units received 2.8 percent of real disposable income. By 2000, the top 1 percent increased its share to 8.8 percent.[1] A recent comprehensive study of Swedish income distribution during the 20th century concluded: "Our findings suggest that top income shares in Sweden, like many other Western countries, decreased significantly over the first eighty years of the century. . . . Most of this decrease happened before 1950, that is, before expansion of the Swedish welfare state. As in many other countries, most of the fall was due to decreasing shares in the very top (the top one percent), while the income share of the lower half of the top decile . . . has been extraordinarily stable. Most of the fall is explained by decreased income from capital" (Roine and Waldenstrom, 2006, p. 24).

Income redistribution is easier for activist states to promise than to achieve. Many countries have tried, but

Roine and Waldenstrom show that the broad contour of the share of the top percentile is very similar in the seven countries they examined. Country efforts to redistribute had much less effect than broad tendencies. All countries experienced a large decline in the share of the top decile from about 1910 to 1980. The range drops from 20 to 25 percent to 5 to 10 percent in 1980. This is followed by a rise. By 2004, major differences appear, perhaps reflecting the importance of new technology and level of educational attainment in different countries. The top decile received about 15 percent in the United States and 13 percent in Canada and the United Kingdom, but about 8 percent in Sweden and 5 percent in the Netherlands. Chart 1.1 shows the decline in the share received by the top percentile.

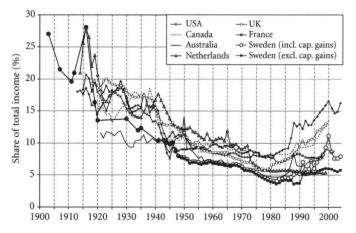

CHART 1.1 *Notes and Sources*: Australia (Atkinson and Leigh, 2006), Canada (Saez and Veall, 2005), France (Piketty, 2003), Netherlands and the United Kingdom (Atkinson and Salverda, 2005), and the United States (Piketty and Saez, 2003).

Data on income distribution have many flaws: people underreport and accurate sampling is difficult; the share of income from capital varies across countries; and people move within the distribution, so the lowest 10 percent and the highest 10 percent are not the same people over time. Careful research on U.S. distribution shows that in 2007 the group with lowest incomes had average wealth that put them in the fourth quintile of the wealth distribution, 61 to 80 percent. Their loss and negative income resulted from business and wealth losses (Diaz-Gimenez et al., 2011, p. 9). The proportion of divorced, separated, or single mothers has increased, with the lowest 10 percent disproportionately of this kind. Their relative poverty cannot be blamed on capitalism, although capitalist growth may have facilitated choices that led to this outcome.

Educational attainment increased in importance to income in the latter part of the 20th century. Low educational attainment and broken family structure are related. The spread in educational attainment works not only to cause growth but to spread the income distribution.

In 2003, the Organization for Economic Cooperation and Development surveyed attitudes and outcomes in the United States and some European countries. Americans worked more hours, experienced substantially lower unemployment rates, and lived in houses with nearly twice the space. The Europeans had much more extensive welfare states, but the Americans were far more satisfied with their lives. When asked: "How satisfied are you with your life?," 57 percent of the Americans answered "very."

In France, Germany, and Italy only 14 to 17 percent gave that answer. Slightly higher percentages answered "not very or not at all." Only 8 percent of Americans gave that answer.

CONCLUSION

Capitalism is not a utopian system, but there is no better system for providing growth and personal freedom. Capitalism's known alternatives offer less freedom and lower growth, and the "better alternatives" people imagine are almost always someone's idea of utopia. Libraries are full of books on utopia, and those that have been tried have either not survived or not flourished. The most common reason for failure is that one person's or one group's utopian ideal is unsatisfactory for others who live subject to its rules. Either the rules change or they are enforced by authorities. Capitalism, particularly democratic capitalism, gains support because it provides a means for orderly change in government. Choice is one of freedom's most valued attributes.

Critics of capitalism seek viable alternatives to support but usually fail to recognize that, unlike socialism, capitalism is adaptive, not rigid. Private ownership of the means of production flourishes regardless of culture. Capitalism's critics have recently discovered Chinese capitalism to propose as an alternative to American capitalism, whose main feature is mercantilism and rigid controls on capital. China's progress exploits international free trade—and the willingness of the United States to run a current account payments deficit. China is more authoritarian than Japan or the West, as Meiji Japan, Korea, and Taiwan also were in the past, and it lacks the rule of law, which is critical for the protection of personal and property rights. Growth produces a middle class, followed by demands for political freedom. China is in the early stages of development following the successful path pioneered by Japan, Korea, Taiwan, Hong Kong, and others who chose export-led growth under trade rules. Sustained economic growth led to social and political freedom in Japan, Korea, and Taiwan. Perhaps China will follow. No country has sustained economic growth without adopting the rule of law. Perhaps China will be the first. More likely it will not. Either freedom will increase as in Korea and Taiwan or growth rates will fall.

A large part of China's high growth rate results from movement of workers from low productivity in agriculture to manufacturing. If Chinese statistics can be believed, mobility from farm to factory accounts for about three-fourths of the growth rate. When that ends, as it will, the Chinese growth rate will decline substantially, as in Japan.

China faces another restriction on future growth. Restrictions on freedom limit innovation. Open democratic capitalist systems generate new ideas, new technologies, and new industries. Restrictions on freedom will limit China's long-term growth by suppressing initiative and innovation. It is not enough to train engineers; progress requires freedom to innovate.

Capitalism continues to spread. Instead of ending, as some critics suppose, capitalism has spread to cultures as different as Brazil, Chile, China, Japan, and Korea. It is the only system humans have found in which personal freedom, progress, and opportunities coexist. Most of the faults and flaws on which critics dwell are human faults, as Immanuel Kant recognized. Capitalism is the only system that adapts to all manner of cultural and institutional differences. It continues to spread and adapt and will continue to do so for the foreseeable future as long as people value both growth and freedom.

NOTES

1   Source: Statistics Sweden.

REFERENCES

Diaz-Gimenez, J., A. Glover, A., and J.-V. Rios-Rull. 2011. "Facts on the Distribution of Earnings, Income, and Wealth in the United States: 2007 Update." *Quarterly Review*, 34, Federal Reserve Bank of Minneapolis, February, 2–31.

Gwartney, J., and R. Larson. 1996. *Economic Freedom of the World.* Washington, DC: Cato Institute.

Hayek, Friedrich (1944). *The Road to Serfdom.* Chicago, University of Chicago Press.

Kant, Immanuel. 1784. "Ideas for a Universal History with a Cosmopolitan Purpose." Quoted in Isaiah Berlin (1990), *The Crooked Timber of Humanity: Chapters in the History of Ideas.* Princeton: Princeton University Press.

Meltzer, A. H., and Scott F. Richard. 1981. "A Rational Theory of the Size of Government." *Journal of Political Economy*, 89 (October), 914–927.

Peltzman, Sam. (2004). *Regulation and the Natural Progress of Opulence.* Washington, DC: AEI-Brookings Joint Center for Regulatory Studies.

Popper, Karl (1945). *The Open Society and Its Enemies.* London: Routledge.

Roine, Joseph, and Daniel Waldenstrom. 2006. "The Evolution of Top Incomes in an Egalitarian Society: Sweden, 1903–2004." Stockholm: Stockholm School of Economics, unpublished.

Thatcher, Margaret (1993). *The Downing Street Years.* New York: Harper Collins.

2

REGULATION AND THE

WELFARE STATE

FOR MOST OF the 20th century, socialism was the main alternative to capitalism. Varieties ranged from democratic socialism in Great Britain to rigidly authoritarian socialism in the Soviet Union and China. All failed. And with the exceptions of Cuba and North Korea, all have been replaced. Most became tyrannies, jailing or murdering opponents—none produced sustained growth. For most, the experience of socialism forever destroyed the world's earlier romantic belief that socialism would bring justice and fairness.

Of course, socialism's failure did not end political demands for justice and fairness. Those who favor redistribution and regulation finally recognized that capitalism produced growth in incomes and living standards and increased the funds available for redistribution. Capitalism's critics changed tack by replacing their demand for state ownership of industry with demands for an increased share of earnings and income to be taxed and redistributed and more regulation of private decisions.

As far back as the 1830s, Alexis de Tocqueville warned of the threat to democratic government from rising demands for redistribution, predicting that, if left unchecked, these demands would lead to higher taxes and less investment, growth, and progress. By the early 21st century, all institutions analysts recognized that U.S. debt and deficits were unsustainable and threatened to bring on a crisis.

REGULATION

Early regulations sought to provide public goods when markets failed to do so. Police protection is the classic example. In principle, everyone pays taxes to hire police, who serve the community. National defense is an easy extension. Traffic rules are another. Economists recognize that public goods require collective action to supplement markets.

Regulation has grown from these early beginnings in developed countries to cover banking and finance, the environment, consumer products, drugs and alcohol, and much else. Demands for regulation often follow on the heels of any controversy over widespread private malfeasance, dishonesty, and self-dealing. However, as Kant observed: periodically, failures will occur and dishonesty will be found. Once in place, regulation is rarely removed. Regulation comes to serve the regulators, as well as constituencies that control it and benefit from it. But regulation is often circumvented.

Years ago, Sam Peltzman pointed out that regulation made some medicines safer but delayed or prevented the use of others. He recommended a light regulatory hand, so that a drug would be made available for those who needed it, whenever the net benefits clearly outweighed the risks. The regulator, the Food and Drug Administration, never heeded his advice. In part, it prioritized its own bureaucratic concerns. For to authorize a drug that helps some but risks side effects for others means that it is still too easy for an attention-seeking press, or grandstanding members of Congress, to paint each new report of harm as a case that could have been avoided. Such episodes then spur calls for ever more regulation, as well as for changes in political leadership.

The financial crisis of 2008 brought enormous political pressure for more regulation—despite regulation's failure in the first instance to have foreseen, prevented, or moderated any of these events. A deluge of journalism blamed financial sector greed, risky instruments such as "derivatives," and deregulation. Others attributed the crisis to government housing policy, especially promotion of no-down-payment mortgages to borrowers who lacked credit history. Both bankers and regulators made mistakes and errors of judgment. The Federal Reserve had representatives from its regulatory staff resident in large banks to monitor securities and loans well before the crisis. They did not prevent banks from making risky loans or circumventing regulation. Greed is a human failure, not a systemic one. Regulation can never fully eliminate greed—only change its locus.

Many mistakes were made, by bankers, borrowers, and government officials, but as Napoleon Bonaparte is said to have advised: "Never ascribe to malice that which is adequately explained by incompetence." Regulation failed. As Kant reminds us, humans are imperfect and they make mistakes. In this case, government housing policy and the policy of preventing failures by large financial institutions encouraged large risk-taking by some bankers, which led to disaster. Some bankers clearly made mistakes. Had the federal government mortgage lenders and the loosening of mortgage standards not encouraged home ownership by low-income households, the crisis probably would not have happened—normally functioning markets would not have financed a massive increase in loans with no down payment.

They were encouraged by the too-big-to-fail policy and later by the willingness of government financial corporations to purchase low-quality mortgages.

The crisis was avoidable. After rescuing the remains of failed investment bank Bear Stearns in March by selling it to J.P. Morgan Chase and purchasing assets that Morgan would not take, in October the Federal Reserve reversed the too-big-to-fail (TBTF) policy it had followed since the 1970s. For years the Federal Reserve prevented failure by large banks, and increasingly other smaller nonbanks such as Long-term Capital and Bear Stearns. Markets interpreted the assistance to Bear Stearns as evidence that TBTF would continue. Then, without warning, the Treasury and the Federal Reserve ended TBTF policy in October 2008 by letting Lehman Brothers fail. Market uncertainty soared. What would the regulators do next? Panic spread worldwide within a few days, as no one could be sure what would happen to financial firms that had borrowed heavily.

The Federal Reserve and Treasury quickly reversed policy by lending to prevent AIG, a large insurance company, from failing. The Federal Reserve responded aggressively to the panic by lending large amounts to keep credit markets operating. Its actions prevented a financial collapse.

The Federal Reserve has never in its long history either announced to the public or followed a rule governing its lender-of-last-resort function. The desirability of a rule—a policy that markets know and expect to be followed—is well known, and the absence of one increases uncertainty. It also encourages failing firms to seek aid from political bodies. More than 100 years ago, Walter Bagehot urged the Bank of England to announce its lender-of-last-resort rule. After the Bank did so, failures did not become crises. Banks understood that their survival at times depended on holding marketable collateral acceptable for discount at the central bank. By failing to announce a lender-of-last-resort rule, the Federal Reserve magnified the crisis. Later proposals for regulatory changes then proposed to end TBTF. The Dodd-Frank law in 2010 authorized the secretary of the treasury to decide TBTF during a future financial crisis. No treasury secretary should be expected to opt for failure in the middle of a crisis. And the same legislation included funds to pay for bailouts, thus allowing large banks to anticipate rescue before failure. This promotes risk-taking and moral hazard.

Bank equity capital deters excessive risk-taking by requiring the bank to pay for its portfolio mistakes and unforeseen changes in external circumstances out of its own capital. If regulators raised capital requirements, bank stockholders would bear the risk of mistakes, which would encourage prudence. Taxpayers would not pay for bankers' errors.

In the 1920s, large banks held about a 20 percent ratio of reserves to assets. TBTF policy and deposit insurance contributed to the large banks reducing reserve ratios to 8 percent or below. Raising capital requirements is the obvious way to shift financial risk back to bank managers and investors. Central bankers meeting in Switzerland agreed on higher capital requirements, and some foreign governments adopted substantially higher capital requirements. The preliminary report of the United Kingdom's Banking Commission recognized that increased capital in British banks would protect the public and the economy.

Bank regulators are charged with protecting the public and overseeing risks to the system as a whole. That's the reason all countries have some form of deposit insurance by law or custom. A policy that allows any bank to become too big to fail shifts losses onto the taxpaying public. Instead of protecting the public, regulations protect large banks, by bailing out their losses. The public pays the cost of the bailouts in taxes. Large-bank borrowing costs decline relative to other banks, such as the small and medium-sized ones that are still allowed to fail. Bankers learn to grow large to obtain regulator protection from failure and lower borrowing costs.

Earlier in economic history, all banks that became insolvent were allowed to fail. To protect the public and avoid the spread of failure to banks that held claims against the failing bank, banks in a crisis would be permitted to borrow on good collateral from the central bank. There were no bailouts. To reassure the public about safety (a matter about which individuals should always retain some measure of caveat emptor), banks posted their capital and surplus prominently on their windows. Both were higher than under recent too-big-to-fail policy. This not only protected the public, it also reduced failures.

In the light of this history and recent experience, elimination of TBTF and improvement in mortgage and housing policies seem obvious policy improvements. Months of discussion and consideration in Congress produced legislation that institutionalized TBTF and made no changes in mortgage or housing policies. The secretary of the treasury heads a council that has the final decision. In the past, the secretary of the treasury has been a leading advocate of TBTF. The new legislation gives the secretary no incentive to change.

There are several reasons regulations fail. Two of the more prominent are capture (of the regulators) and circumvention (of laws meant to restrain risky, or bad, behavior). Capture occurs when the regulated become the regulators, or when regulators plan to make a lucrative career change by joining the industry they hitherto had been regulating. The Securities and Exchange Commission (SEC) is famous for the extent of movement between regulator and regulated. The SEC is not alone. Regulators often look for people with detailed knowledge of their subject. The regulated industry is a likely source, so it is not unusual to find people moving back and forth. The Federal Reserve is a training ground for bank and financial market economists. The Internal Revenue Service is a training ground for tax accountants. The list is long.

The problem is that the people who write the laws and regulations the private sector must follow are in an excellent position to advise the regulated firms. Some are scrupulous, but as Kant warned, some are not. During the years of rising inflation in the 1970s, savings and loan associations operated under numerous regulations that limited the assets they could buy and the interest rates they could pay. Inflation had a devastating effect. Earnings came from a portfolio of long-term mortgages with fixed interest payments. The thrifts financed the portfolio by acquiring short-term deposits.

The business was very profitable when mortgage interest rates remained above the rate paid on deposits. Inflation reversed the relation, eliminating profits and introducing large losses. In an effort to help the industry, Congress approved a "regulatory accounting standard," which tried to hide the losses. Regulation and other assistance extended the life of many thrift associations but also increased the losses that the public paid after the thrifts failed. The net cost to taxpayers was about $150 billion. The savings and loan industry almost disappeared, a victim of inflation and bad regulation.

In 1937, Congress created the Federal National Mortgage Association (FNMA) to improve the liquidity of the mortgage market by creating a market and offering to buy mortgages from lenders. By 2005, FNMA had become the largest purchaser of very risky subprime and Alt-A mortgages. These purchases supported government programs to encourage home ownership by low-income earners. Government agencies authorized mortgages that required no down payment to borrowers who had no credit history. Defaults on such mortgages were large. Taxpayers will lose $400 billion, according to the Congressional Budget Office, the largest loss on any government program to date. It does not require great financial acumen to understand that issuing no-down-payment loans to people without a good credit record is a risky enterprise. Large losses should be expected. This is another example of regulatory failure abetted by bankers who made the risky loans. Well-intentioned action to expand home ownership produced a financial and economic disaster.

The influence of lobbyists and special pleading makes a mockery of claims to fairness. The Internal Revenue Service in the United States administers the federal income tax. The tax law states that income is taxed from "whatever source derived." Then follow hundreds of pages of exceptions. In 1986, President Reagan and Congress agreed to reduce marginal tax rates by closing many exemptions and special privileges. In a few years, many of the privileges returned and marginal rates rose.

If individuals were like Plato's ideal, devoted to public well-being and committed to their task for life, regulations might provide the justice and fairness that proponents promise. But Kant is a better judge of mankind than Plato. Some in both the private and public sectors will be dishonest, corrupt, or self-serving. And some will make mistakes.

Napoleon warned that we should not neglect incompetence. The SEC was told several times that Bernard Madoff could not be investing as he claimed. Detailed demonstration of this point to SEC officials had no effect. Those at the SEC responsible for preventing fraud did not understand what they were shown. Investors with Madoff lost billions of dollars in aggregate.

To increase home sales during the recovery from the 2007–09 recession, the Treasury offered purchasers a tax credit. Government investigators found subsequently that 1,300 prison inmates received more than $9 million of tax credits despite being in jail at the time they applied. Some of the inmates (240) were serving life sentences. Napoleon's explanation seems apt.

In 2010, Congress investigated the bailout of American International Group (AIG). In 2008, the Federal Reserve advanced $180 million to avoid AIG's bankruptcy by using a little known provision of the Banking Act called Section 13(3) that became part of the Federal Reserve's authority during the Great Depression. The original purpose was to provide credit to small and medium-sized businesses that banks would not service during the Great Depression. Lending to a giant insurer stretched legal authority.

Testifying about the bailout, two treasury secretaries, Henry Paulson and his successor, Timothy Geithner, said that their only choice was to help AIG avoid failure or suffer another Great Depression. Neither secretary mentioned that classical central banking offered a third alternative—let AIG fail but open the discount window wide by making loans to all borrowers who offered good collateral. Again, regulators protected the failing firm at taxpayer's expense instead of protecting the public.

Failures of regulators and regulation are not limited to financial regulation. Prohibition failed to eliminate drinking alcohol but left crime syndicates behind. The War on Drugs failed to limit the use of narcotics, but it strengthened criminal groups and created havoc in Mexico and on our border. Illegal immigration continues despite public concern and frequent promises to slow or end it.

An economist can defend special treatment for banks because public authorities supply a public good by protecting the payments system. If the banking system, or a large part of the system, fails, payments are disrupted. Economic activity depends on payments for transactions. That reasoning supports deposit insurance and, along with it, banking regulation to limit risk taking. It does not support too-big-to-fail. The regulator must prevent the spread of failures to otherwise solvent institutions. That's the role of the lender-of-last-resort—to prevent failures from spreading by lending on good collateral. A clearly stated rule encourages prudence and limits risk taking. The Federal Reserve continues to operate without a rule that limits what it can do. It has become subject to pressures from the administration and the Congress to bail out failures and inflate and depreciate the dollar.

In the 2007–08 financial crisis, regulators made large loans to prevent financial failures. Many people then argued that if financial firms, including some that contributed to the crises, received assistance to prevent insolvency, why not extend public protection to other firms, including Chrysler, General Motors, and AIG, to save jobs.

Protection of the payments system preserves an external benefit on which trade and commerce depends. The automobile industry and others cannot make that claim. Further, there is no systemic issue involved. If General Motors were bankrupt, its principal assets—its manufacturing plants— would be sold. Financial losses and a temporary loss of output would occur, but the physical capital would remain. Further, domestic automobile and truck production would continue at Ford, Toyota, Honda, and other foreign transplants.

The lasting effect of widespread protection from failure is that companies are encouraged to become large enough to be protected. Too-big-to-fail spreads from finance to other industries. Some are encouraged to take excessive risks; a response economists call "moral hazard" increases. Also, protection of failing companies removes the strong discipline of the capitalist system. Instead of transferring capital from failing to growing firms and industries, protection shifts capital toward weaker enterprises. Regulators lose sight of the fact that capitalism without failure is like religion without sin. It works badly or fails to work for public benefit.

From experience as diverse as prohibition of alcoholic beverages under the Volstead Act in the 1920s to the international agreement to prevent countries from developing nuclear weapons or other instruments of mass destruction, we should have learned that regulations and prohibitions are not easily enforced. Other examples of failure of regulation could be added. Outlawing cocaine has not prevented addicts from finding "crack houses." It should not surprise anyone that addicts find the house but the police rarely do. The reason is the addicts have a strong incentive but the police have a large disincentive. The criminals who trade in cocaine are likely to kill police who raid their outlets.

Of course, all regulation doesn't fail. Successful regulation will get ordinary human incentives right and channel them in ways realistically enforceable through means a state is competent to accomplish affordably. Regulation might grant a monopoly, restricting entry into the regulated activity to a specific group. Pharmaceutical patents are an example, which reward innovators. All patents create monopoly rights for a limited time. Sometimes, the public monitors and enforces compliance with rules by favoring competitors who follow them.

Regulation fails when, however well-intentioned, it is poorly designed. I have put forward two laws of regulation to explain why regulation often accomplishes less than it promises. First, lawyers and bureaucrats promulgate regulations, but, if they are costly to the regulated, markets will circumvent them. Second, regulations are static whereas markets are dynamic. If regulations are inconvenient or costly, markets will learn to circumvent them, say by capturing the regulator, or carving out exemptions for themselves. Complex laws offer endless ways for effective circumvention, often unnoticed.

Some laws and regulations change the incentives of the regulated, sometimes in ways that those who put the regulation into place do not anticipate. A rule requiring bank capital to increase with bank size changes the costs of getting or staying big, raising the cost to stockholders if management gambles away the company's funds. Complex governing laws or regulations also raise costs of entering and competing in an industry, its "costs of entry." This encourages existing firms to seek to regulate their own industry in order to deter competition.

Regulation may seek laudable ends, but, as Kant so presciently warned, mankind is endlessly self-seeking. Powerful firms contribute to campaigns of both parties. The very dynamism of capitalist economies makes circumvention of regulation likely, as the relative competence and insight of the private sector outstrips that of the public. Capture of the regulators by the regulated has become increasingly common.

For 50 years, developed countries have aided poor countries directly or indirectly through international lenders. The World Bank Group includes the International Development Agency (IDA), a principal source of subsidized loans to developing countries, as well as advice and persuasion to adopt policies and take actions favored by the Bank or the IDA.

These lenders earnestly believe to their core that their ideas for development concepts and regulatory plans will be welfare improving. Yet the Bank and IDA have a poor record of achievement. Some recent books document the failures. Dambiso Moyo (2008), a Zambian economist, and William Easterly (2002) have analyzed the failures of decades of foreign aid. Moyo argues that more than $1 billion in development aid to Africa per year, free money, destroys Africa's incentive to choose among successful development strategies and promotes corruption. Aid to Africa for the past 50 years cost at least $1 trillion. Results are meager. Moyo argues that aid discourages investment and supports corrupt regimes.

Once again, the well-intentioned people who developed aid programs overlooked the perverse incentives they were creating. But incentives determine the outcomes. When countries as diverse as China, India, or Brazil changed development strategy from command and control to market-based incentives, growth rates soared.

At last, in 2009, the World Bank released an evaluation by its Independent Evaluation Group. The study found evidence that the Bank had inadequately addressed the fraud and corruption in its programs of which outside observers had complained for years. Aid programs aren't hopeless, but incentives for progress must be part of any such plan, and local leaders (who ascertainably don't primarily stand to benefit from the programs personally) must agree that any plan must incorporate open markets and competition to encourage and sustain growth.

Regulation and redistribution cause special interest groups to spring up, which then seek to influence allocation. There are countless examples in agriculture, health care, education, and wherever resources are directed by regulation. Deals made between government and special interests can ignore, or ill-serve, the public interest. Instead of letting individuals decide for themselves, regulation often redistributes to those who are best organized or those who contribute the most to political campaigns.

Striking examples of successful reforms aren't hard to find. An example from the United States is the 1994 decision to change the welfare program intended to help low-income households, especially female-headed households. The change introduced incentives. To get benefits, recipients had to work or train for work. The result was dramatic. Millions went to work, learned skills, and gained incentives to improve their lot in life. Participation in the principal welfare program, Aid to Families with Dependent Children, declined by 60 percent nationwide. Incomes of former welfare families increased an average of 25 percent. A side benefit was that children learned that adults work, that earnings are related to effort, that they could be expected to work, and that better jobs required better education. Not everyone benefitted, but many did. Welfare roles dropped, and people who worked became eligible for income supplements from the Earned Income Tax Credit.

Mexico required low-income families to send children to school. If they failed to do so, they lost their transfer payment. The incentive increased schooling. Brazil adopted the same law with similar beneficial results.

Behavioral economics has allowed us to move toward more intelligent styles of regulation that work with individual freedom, or impinge upon it less. As in all behavioral economics, individuals are not assumed to be fully rational, fully informed, or fully aware of all of the implications of their choices (Thaler and Sunstein, 2003). Government regulation is "libertarian paternalism" whereby a regulator can avoid irrational choices by choosing more wisely than (some) individuals. Cigarette taxes are an example.

No doubt sometimes regulators can introduce incentives that change the choices that individuals make, but the Kantian principle is at work here as elsewhere. I know no reason to believe that paternalistic choice will remain limited or that it will not be abused to achieve ends the public does not share.

AN EXAMPLE OF REGULATORY REFORM

The credit market and housing crisis that began in August 2007 created demands for new regulation of financial markets. After intense discussion, Congress, in July 2010, passed a gigantic new law that regulated consumer credit, hedge funds, banks, and other financial institutions. Proponents hailed the bill as landmark legislation.

The crisis stimulated much discussion of its causes. Not much agreement was found. Some cited bankers, mortgage bankers, and other financial intermediaries. Others cited loose monetary policy and government housing and mortgage policies. President Obama appointed a commission to hear witnesses and report by December 2010.

Congress didn't wait for the report to enact regulation. As is so often the case, the legislation left several hundred decisions to regulators. This opened opportunities for interest groups to lobby actively for weaker or stronger rules. What the legislation did and how its costs and burdens would sort out couldn't be ascertained until after it had been made law—or after court constitutional challenges of various provisions.

The bill was packed with matters that had nothing to do with the financial crisis but served individual legislators' agendas. For example, the law regulated hedge funds despite any evidence or credible claim that hedge funds had any relationship to the crisis whatsoever. Proponents of gender and racial quotas inserted new requirements directed at their concerns. These are but a few of the provisions that special interest groups imposed.

As the cliché goes, "mistakes were made." Bankers, other types of firms acting in a similar financial capacity such as insurance giant AIG, the public, and especially regulators, all made mistakes. Federal Reserve policy remained too expansive. Long before the crisis, Federal Reserve banks had its examiners placed in the largest commercial banks, yet the Federal Reserve never challenged anything about their lending policies—or their circumvention of Basel rules requiring banks to post more capital to conduct activities of the risk level they were engaging in. Federal housing policy promoted lending to low-income families without good credit histories and imposed no down payment requirements. The quasigovernmental lending institutions Fannie Mae and Freddy Mac made markets in these loans, the enormous extent of which sent both into insolvency. They are now in receivership, their portfolios guaranteed by taxpayers. The largest banks and bank holding companies were protected against failure by the too-big-to-fail policy.

The massive financial reform did little or nothing to correct these errors and failures. The Federal Reserve acquired even more new regulatory powers. TBTF stayed in place. Instead of requiring increased bank capital, a council headed by the secretary of the treasury was given the power to decide in individual situations, meaning that all such decisions would be political. Though the problems with housing policy and Fannie and Freddy are widely recognized, nothing was done about either. Instead of putting housing subsidies on the budget, as proper procedure requires, the new legislation added still more off-budget funding for consumer regulation. The new consumer finance agency can draw on the Federal Reserve. Instead of paying 90 percent of its surplus to the Treasury, the Federal Reserve will now finance the demands of the consumer regulator.

Like most prior regulation, this new legislation fails to incorporate incentives directed to desired outcomes. It will not achieve a safer, sounder financial system. In his discussion of the economic functions of the constitution, Pejovic (2008) shows the need for constitutional restrictions on the power of regulators.

REDISTRIBUTION

Unrestricted capitalism lets markets determine how income is distributed. No modern democratic capitalist system accepts that outcome. Democracy permits voters to tax and redistribute income.

Our political-economic system is known as a welfare state or mixed economy. In this kind of state, most government activity in the economy produces goods or services that could be, and often are, produced privately—national defense being a notable exception. Education, health care, and pensions, like other services, are produced using capital and labor. The reason for government involvement is said to be redistribution of the costs of these goods, so that people with low incomes can receive these services free or at lower cost. Subsidies encourage overuse and waste, reducing any such program's efficiency, but many of the subsidies go to middle-class voters, not, as alleged, the poor. Many governments promise benefits, such as employee pensions, to be paid in the future that do not affect current budgets. Today, American cities and states are just starting to own up to the costs they have promised in the past, and most are unprepared.

Some estimates of future state and local pension commitments run as high as 3 trillion dollars—mostly guarantees of income for life, based on the retiree's last year of earnings. The sum has been exaggerated by overtime tacked on in the final years.

In many cities in America today, the unfunded pension liability is so vast, they face bankruptcy. In bankruptcy, however, all those contracts will be renegotiable.

Cities and states created this problem by offering future benefits to city employees with little oversight—city budgets need not account for the present value of future contract commitments they make. Had they been required to publicize such figures up front, the problem would not have become as large as it is. The city officials who negotiated these pension contracts well knew what they were doing, but also that they would be out of office when the bill came due. Private sector pension plans overall offer far fewer benefits.

Some private sector pensions are also unsustainably rich. But in creating the Pension Benefit Guarantee Corporation (PBGC), the federal government promised to safeguard private pensions by charging companies a premium to insure them, picking up bankrupt firm obligations. PBGC's revenues are now inadequate to fulfill the pension claims for which it is liable, so PBGC, too, has a large unfunded liability—yet another example of government promises unmatched by honest accounting.

Governments have no intrinsic advantage over the private sector in hiring teachers, doctors, nurses, or other professionals, nor any advantage in building schools or hospitals. Rather, they tend to be at a disadvantage, out of lack of expertise, lack of competition, failure to refine their operations, or because they regulate themselves more heavily than the private sector, for example, by requiring regulated firms to hire only unionized workers. One way to accomplish the goal of redistributing the costs of a public service, but still making sure that efficiency-improving, cost-lowering competition among suppliers of the service still exists, is a system of vouchers. In the past, this technique has engendered organized opposition. When government runs any system, its employees often find it easy to capture. State officials also tend not to guard taxpayers' wallets as jealously as if they were their own.

A larger welfare state changes the way resources are used. Unemployment compensation originated in Western Europe to support the unemployed during increasingly severe recessions in the past. This type of payment risks the creation of subsidies for leisure. Unemployment rates reported in Germany, France, and Italy have risen relative to nations where the benefit was smaller, such as Canada and the United States. In the early postwar decades European welfare states were less extensive so unemployment rates were low. Rates climbed to 8 or 10 percent, even in years without recessions. Similarly, when the state subsidizes health care heavily, this reduces private investment in health care at the same time that taxes rise to pay for redistributive subsidies or regulation.

In the early postwar years, until 1980, the principal economies of Western Europe grew faster than the United States, closing the income, output, and productivity gap that had opened up in WWII between them and the United States. Then, as income and output slowed in the large European welfare states, the gap reversed and kept widening. Table 2.1 shows average growth rates computed from data from the Organization for Economic Cooperation and Development (OECD) for six countries over a 26-year period. On average for the period, income in the United States rose 50 percent faster than in France, which had made the political choice of more welfare spending, less work, and higher unemployment. The difference in average growth rates is no more than 1 percent a year, but that 1 percent means that, starting from the same level, average French incomes are one-quarter smaller than U.S. incomes in a generation, approximately the period covered in Table 2.1.

Under the leadership of Prime Minister Thatcher, the United Kingdom sold its nationalized industries and slowed the growth of Britain's welfare state. Instead of subsidizing failing firms to keep jobs in place, Britain let its markets direct resources toward profitable, growing firms offering other jobs. Thatcher's success led even opposition parties who succeeded her to continue her capitalist approach to growth,

Table 2.1

COMPARATIVE ECONOMIC GROWTH RATES

Country	1981–90	1991–2000	2001–06
France	2.36	1.95	1.70
Germany	2.37	2.11	0.97
Italy	2.42	1.39	0.88
United States	3.25	3.30	2.42
United Kingdom	2.66	2.44	2.53
Ireland	3.67	7.06	5.55

Source: OECD.

whereupon the United Kingdom began to close the income gap with its large continental neighbors. German growth slowed as it devoted large resources to integrate the former East Germany and extend its welfare state to the east.

Ireland's story was most remarkable. Its growth rates reached that of the Asian "tigers," reversing Ireland's previous hundred or more years of outbound migration to become a new destination for immigrants, including former residents who returned to share in the new opportunities. Alas, Ireland allowed banks and the property market to expand too much, ending the long expansion. Then they added to their problems by guaranteeing all bank debt. Once again, taxpayers paid for bankers' mistakes.

Democratic capitalism is not a rigid orthodoxy. People will, at different times, choose either more redistribution or less, a larger welfare state with greater redistribution or a smaller public sector and a higher rate of growth. A remarkable feature of democratic capitalism is that its outcomes are relatively stable. There are always critics who favor more redistribution and express concern for unmet "social needs," and others who want lower tax rates, less current redistribution, more growth, and higher future income. But major changes to the system as a whole are infrequent.

Democratic capitalism persists and spreads because it is not a system of imposed morality. It is the only system mankind has discovered that adapts to the mankind that Kant described rather than promising utopia. And it is culturally malleable. Capitalism in Japan differs from capitalism in the United States or China, just as democratic capitalism in Europe differs from capitalism in China, Japan, or the United States.

The experience of Britain and Ireland has been replicated beyond Western Europe. After a coup that replaced the Allende government with one that promoted capitalism, Chile greatly reduced taxes, tariffs, regulation, and inflation. This expanded its exports and output. After a painful transition, during which the military government suppressed political freedom and used reprehensible tactics, Chile experienced growth rates it never had before, sustainably. In 2010, Chile became the first South American country in the club of advanced economies, the Organization of Economic Cooperation and Development, OECD.

Eventually, Brazil followed the Chilean example by adopting capitalist monetary and fiscal reforms, including one that originated in Mexico to cut welfare benefits to mothers whose children were not in school. These moves achieved economic stability and growth for Brazil, starting with the administration of President Cardoso, and gained strength when a former radical labor union leader, Lula, upon assuming the presidency, implemented still more such reforms. Capitalist measures achieved the growth rates and stability that eluded those who promised justice and fairness.

The most extreme change was China's. After Mao died, his successor, Deng, recognized that Japan, Korea, and the countries of the Chinese diaspora that had followed capitalism achieved sustained growth in living standards, output, and productivity. These countries had invited in foreign investors and competed with their products in world markets. Under Deng, China adopted a large part of capitalist growth strategy. Foreign investors brought productivity improvements, and membership in the World Trade Organization opened additional foreign markets to Chinese products. By following the export-led growth program pioneered by Japan, China released hundreds of millions from poverty. Millions of peasants left rural agriculture to work in the growing industrial sector, just as they had years earlier in Japan and Korea. Capitalism, though limited, achieved reductions in poverty that foreign aid, Communism, and centralized planning had failed to do.

China's experience wasn't lost on its neighbor India. Years of applying the version of socialism India's leaders had learned as students at the London School of Economics had left India mired in a web of bureaucracy, regulation, and restrictions that became known jocularly as the Hindu rate of growth—about 2 percent. Reforms removing some restrictions and opening the economy to trade and investment allowed the growth rate to rise. India's high-quality technical education permitted Indian firms to compete effectively in world markets. As growth increased, millions rose from poverty. India's transformation, like Japan's, showed that market-oriented reforms are possible in a democratic country as well as an authoritarian one.

Market opening and capitalist methods worked where the World Bank and other so-called development institutions had failed. Hundreds of billions of dollars in "aid," directed by well-meaning but misguided development officials, did much less to reduce poverty than a few years of market-based decisions by individuals seeking profits.

Capitalist development produces change. Change is often difficult for those who are affected by it either directly or indirectly. The World Bank and other development agencies attempt to assist governments. But unless there is local support for change, and local people willing to lead that change, development programs often fail.

Comparisons of comparative growth in North and South Korea, the former West and East Germany, and China before reform and the Chinese Diaspora in Singapore, Taiwan, and Hong Kong provide a clear lesson. Welfare states and socialism promise fairness but achieve neither more justice nor higher living standards. Most often, they fail to benefit the poor.

But this lesson is lost on the World Bank and most development agencies. They do not teach that capitalist development is a successful strategy for reducing poverty and increasing growth. The World Bank, especially, is bogged down by corruption in client countries and a consistent failure to introduce programs that maintain incentives and encourage individuals to invest and take risks for future returns (Easterly, 2002).

Kant's warning is at least as relevant to government agencies and nongovernmental institutions as to the private sector. The long history of the Soviet Union and its satellites, and of most African countries, shows the corruption, low growth rates, and absence of freedom that occurs when government takes the major role in managing resources. Capitalism does not guarantee or achieve an end to corruption, but competition and open markets work to reduce it.

Governments have a role in promoting growth and living standards—they are responsible for safeguarding the political infrastructure under which savings can best increase and generate productive investment. Governments exist to foster property rights and freedom of choice, encourage competition internally, where possible, and externally (free trade abroad), facilitate growth by providing quality education (South Korea's postwar record of educating millions has been spectacular), maintain the rule of law, and reduce uncertainty about the future. Reducing uncertainty about the future encourages investment, which is a type of prediction about the future.

Income redistribution must tax some to benefit others. How can taking be justified? A distinguished Harvard philosophy professor, John Rawls, made a popular defense of income redistribution. Rawls recognized that modern ethical theories did not provide a foundation. In his *Theory of Justice* (Rawls, 1971) and later works, he defended redistribution as a moral choice made in the interest of social harmony, but he recognized that people would not voluntarily agree on what he believed was the proper choice. To achieve what he called "justice as fairness," he proposed that the decision about desirable redistribution should be made before anyone knew whether he would be rich or poor. In effect, a constitution would bind all future generations to the redistribution set "behind the veil of ignorance." Those who favored greater equality of outcome applauded Rawls' work.

Rawls' argument is static. It fails to allow the people living today to revise the constitutional agreement made by people who lived long ago. In practice, the rich and poor are not ignorant of their position. They know who they are, and they use that information when they vote for taxation and redistribution. Their notions of justice and fairness differ. People do not accept all constraints made in the past as binding for all time. They think about how government can serve their interests and often the interests of succeeding generations.

Rawls' effort fails to provide a useful analytic defense of redistribution. It denies voters the right to choose taxation and spending and to opt for redistribution or growth. Democratic governments permit choice based on the political decisions of voters concerned about their own welfare and the welfare of their children, grandchildren, and members of their community.

LESSONS FOR THE UNITED STATES

No country has shown greater ability than the United States to sustain growth and freedom over long periods. But the pressure on government to redistribute income that prevails in all capitalist democracies has today produced massive debt, bringing government spending to new peacetime highs. Those who favored such programs use familiar claims about justice and fairness to promote current consumption at the expense of the future. Every society has a constituency that will prefer current spending and redistribution to future value achieved by productive investment and economic growth. Constitutional protections of property rights do not prevent redistribution policies from being legally enacted in response to these constituencies. Pressures for such redistribution rise with aggregate income and with the spread in relative incomes (Meltzer and Richard, 1981).

Data suggest that the relative incomes of those in the lowest income decile aren't much changed by welfare programs. One main reason is family breakup; single mothers are one of the main groups with persistently low incomes. And many of the children from broken families acquire little incentive to learn and gain marketable skills.

As I have argued, regulation and redistribution often fail to achieve the results in justice and equity promised by their sponsors, which so often prove empty. That said, widely shared goals can be pursued—so long as people fully appreciate their costs. Yet some of what is done in response to crises, or to support some popular program, undermines the rule of law. For instance, to increase homeownership or college financing, Congress established lending programs off budget, essentially hiding the cost and thus exaggerating the apparent benefit. Direct subsidies of lending to college students voted on as part of the budget would have been more honest than an off-budget loan program conducted by private sector banks protected by a full U.S. taxpayer guarantee.

Federally subsidized loans to students defer the cost of an education and reduce the immediate costs to the student. This artificially increases demand but tends to inflate those same tuition costs. "Affirmative action" programs similarly facilitate minority enrollment in prestigious universities—an example of regulated "fairness" to redistribute opportunity— but many who benefit from affirmative action programs are not prepared for the standards they face at the best colleges and universities and drop out of school. Would they have benefitted more under a less demanding curriculum? Why do we continue to tolerate the poor quality of much public education? Many proponents of justice and fairness resist changes that might lead to improvements; teachers are not immune from self-interest.

During the 19th and early 20th centuries, the public school system educated millions of immigrant children, many of whom became doctors, lawyers, accountants, engineers, teachers, and other professionals because they had concerned parents who inculcated self-discipline in their children. Many Chinese, Korean, Indian, and other immigrants currently preserve educational values lacking in other homes. To increase incentives for self-improvement, family structure, from which self-discipline is incubated, should be strengthened. Welfare reform, which replaced welfare with work, is an example. Another is the Mexican program that pays mothers only if the children attend school.

After much heated discussion, President Obama was able to push through major legislation in his effort to increase social "fairness"—an expansion of government control over health care. Like most political meanings of "fairness," the bill redistributed costs of health care, with recipients (32 million individuals who did not carry health insurance) gaining at the expense of those who did previously pay into the private insurance system. The bill increased demand for primary care physicians but did nothing to increase their supply. Primary care physicians will now gain patients who previously received care in hospital emergency centers, where they often waited for service; whether primary care physicians can handle this new business better or at less cost overall remains to be seen.

The same legislation substantially increased Medicaid benefits. Medicaid provides services to the poor; its costs are shared among state and federal governments. Many state governments run large budget deficits, especially in California and New York, but elsewhere as well. More spending on health care will have to be met by higher taxes or cuts in education, police, firefighting, and other programs that voters and legislatures will be reluctant or unwilling to make. To avoid reductions in state spending, the federal government transferred billions of dollars to the states in 2009, thus temporarily picking up these rising state costs at the expense of an already unsustainable federal budget deficit.

Hailed by many as a great achievement, the Obama health care bill nevertheless used false estimates of future costs, so the next step in the health debate must be to deal with the new law's enormous increase in the future unfunded liability. Reducing this cost is likely to come from some combination of higher taxes and smaller benefits. The market will adjust to this new law. Like any system of price controls, government control of medical payments will produce distortions. Medicare, for example, has attempted to effect savings by reducing payments to physicians, causing some to withdraw from the program. "Concierge medicine," under which doctors charge a limited number of private patients an annual fee, and other such substitutions are likely to expand as controls and regulations increase.

Health care is not alone. Both political parties are responsible for the unsustainable increase in government spending that the health care bill exemplifies. The future will differ from the past. Some combination of higher tax rates, reduced spending, and a higher age to receive pensions or Medicare will be required to solve unsustainable deficits and mounting debt. The solution's mix will be the subject of intense negotiation, but as fiscal crisis looms, officials will find one. In 2011 the negotiation started.

Resolving the current deficit and debt expansion won't be easy. The system needs a way to limit the urge to spend more than future taxpayers can pay. Debt allows the current generation to grant itself benefits without taxing themselves, shifting cost to future generations who have no current voice. For many decades, two rules maintained discipline. The public adherence to the gold standard rule of monetary restraint, and the balanced budget rule of fiscal restraint in peacetime. Agreement on rules for monetary and fiscal policies will be necessary to prevent future crises. If enforced, rules restrain all parties to achieve a common benefit, stability.

Congress also passes laws delegating to unelected civil servants the right to specify regulatory details. This opens opportunities for corruption and bribery. All regulation doesn't have this effect, but Kant's rule applies as much or more to regulated as to competitive markets. Further, much regulation bypasses the rule of law by substituting administrative decisions for general rules.

When I served as an acting member of the president's council of economic advisers in 1988, one of my duties, at times, was to recommend whether the president should sign or veto new legislation. One piece of legislation was the Insider Trading Act of 1988. The central issue about insider trading is how valuable information can be transferred to third parties. Efficient markets depend on the way information becomes available. The proposed legislation did not offer a definition of an illegal transfer of new information. That left interpretation of the law's main restriction to prosecutors and courts who could choose how it was used and against whom. I proposed that the president veto the bill. Alas, the president's chief of staff had committed the president, so the bill became law, another neglect of the rule of law.

CONCLUSION

The regulated welfare state is the redistributionists' solution to the problems that arise in a capitalist system. Restricting capitalism illustrates that most of the alleged deficiencies are personal, not structural, as Kant recognized centuries ago.

My aim in this chapter has been to show that much regulation invites corruption, arbitrary decisions, and circumvention. Regulation is more likely to succeed if it changes the incentives faced by the regulated. One of many examples is pharmaceutical regulation; it offers patent protection, so it creates temporary monopolies that are profitable to producers. They willingly defend and enforce their monopoly.

All systems redistribute income. The chart in chapter 1 earlier showed that redistributive policies are rarely powerful. They work best in relatively homogeneous populations where most agree on desirable social outcomes, as in the Nordic countries, or Japan.

Proponents of increased regulation or income redistribution rarely mention their long-term effects. Heavy regulation in India brought corruption and slow growth. Loosening regulation in Chile, India, China, and elsewhere was followed by an economic growth surge and sustained growth. Large-scale redistribution can discourage work and thus slow growth. Politicians in many countries promised larger pensions and health care spending than countrymen were willing to pay.

Drawing more resources into regulation and redistribution lowers growth and future income. Discretion and an administrator's judgment replace the rule of law. The United States avoided large expenditures for regulation through most of its history because it followed a fiscal rule of restricting unbalanced budgets to wartimes, and repaying that debt when peace returned. A 21st-century fiscal rule is a discipline we now need.

REFERENCES

Easterly, William. (2002). *The Elusive Quest for Growth: Economist's Adventures and Misadventures in the Tropics.* Cambridge, MA: MIT Press.

Meltzer, Allan H., and Scott F. Richard. (1981). "A Rational Theory of the Size of Government." *Journal of Political Economy*, 89 (October): 914–927.

Moyo, Dambiso. (2008). *Dead Aid: Destroying the Biggest Global Myth of Our Time.* New York: Farrar, Straus and Giroux.

Pejovic, Svetozar. (2008). *Law, Informal Rules and Economic Performance.* Cheltenham, UK: Edward Elgar.

Rawls, John. (1971). *A Theory of Justice.* Cambridge: Belknap Press for Harvard University Press.

Thaler, Richard H. and Cass R. Sunstein. (2003). "Libertarian Paternalism Is Not an Oxymoron." *University of Chicago Law Review*, 30: 1159–1202.

3

WHY BIG DEFICITS NOW?

THE UNITED STATES government is on course in 2009, 2010, and 2011 to run the largest peacetime deficits in its history—at least $1 trillion a year for ten years or more—with no end in sight. Logic, and history, tell us that financing such enormous deficits will cause inflation and a depreciation of the dollar against other currencies. Every knowledgeable observer agrees that the projected deficits and debt are unsustainable. Studies at the Bank for International Settlements suggest that decades of surpluses will be required to restore the 2007 debt to GDP ratio (Cecchetti et al., 2010, p. 12).

It is a big problem, but not a new one. Historically, politicians give lip service to fiscal restraint. Today, however, efforts to achieve budget balance or surplus in the United States are a rarity—apart from routine complaints from the party currently out of office about deficits attributed to their opponent. Once in office, the winner neglects fiscal orthodoxy and adds to the deficit. Although the 2010 election shows considerable public concern about spending, there are only two post–World War II exceptions to continued deficits: the Eisenhower and Clinton presidencies. Over the term of his presidency, Eisenhower achieved a balanced budget, though he ran a high (for the time) deficit during the 1957–58 recession.

From President Washington to the Civil War, except for years of war, the federal government ran surpluses 75 percent of the time. Alexander Hamilton, the country's first Treasury Secretary, paid off Revolutionary War debts but ran budget deficits in three of the first eight years of the new republic. Other peacetime deficits in our history have occurred during recessions. During the War of 1812, total outstanding gross debt rose from $45 million to a maximum of $127 million. By the early 1830s, the federal government had retired almost all outstanding debt.[1] As in most wars, Civil War expenditures greatly exceeded revenues. The $1.3 million in government spending in 1865 was more than 20 times government spending in the last pre-war year, 1860. By war's end, the nation's gross debt had reached $2.7 billion. The federal budget remained in surplus for the next 28 years. By 1892, gross debt was below $100 million. Despite the surpluses, or perhaps because they encouraged private investment, the economy grew.

During World War I, federal government deficits totaled $23 billion for the years 1917–19 and were $25 billion by war's end. In the 1920s Treasury Secretary Andrew Mellon reduced tax rates and controlled spending. By 1930, gross debt had fallen to $16 billion.

That was the end of sustained effort to reduce government debt. During the Great Depression and World War II, the budget was in deficit every year. By war's end, 1946, gross debt reached $269 billion, and in the following years, avoiding postwar deflation and unemployment took priority over debt reduction. President Truman raised tax rates to finance most Korean War spending. President Eisenhower, who spoke often about fiscal responsibility and balanced budgets, ran several budget surpluses. From 1946 to 1957, gross debt rose little, except during the deep 1957–58 recession.

Today, government spending has increased greatly. At the beginning of the 20th century, the federal government spent 2.8 percent of total output (GNP). In World War I, as in all wars, spending and taxes increased. By 1929, spending was 3.7 percent of GNP. From the mid-1980s to the present government spending has fluctuated around 18 percent of GNP. In 2010, it was 25 percent of GNP. If the current large gap between revenues and expenditures is to be closed, taxes are likely to rise. Future unfunded liabilities add to the pressure for higher taxes when they are spent and debt service increases spending, as well as the total debt.

In the past, when the nation spent more than it collected in tax, it was to finance wars. When the war ended, deficit spending ended. Today's deficits continue and grow in size, but defense and military spending, though large, are a greatly reduced share of spending. The big increases are for social welfare programs and redistribution.

After World War II, military spending related to the Cold War drove government spending, but military spending as a percentage of total government spending has since declined. The main driver of government spending since the mid-1960s has not been military spending, but regulation and income redistribution in the form of entitlements— Social Security, Medicare/Medicaid, and welfare. Estimates in 2009 of future medical costs exceeded expected revenues ("unfunded liabilities"), for which the government is liable, by $60 trillion or more.

From 1961 through 1977, the government budget was in deficit; government spent more than it received in tax revenues during every year except 1969. President Johnson borrowed heavily to finance increased social spending and the war in Vietnam. Gross debt reached $369 billion when he left office. President Nixon did more of the same. Domestic spending by governments rose rapidly. By the 1980s, deficits of $150 to $250 billion had become common (Council of Economic Advisors, 2008). President Reagan slowed the growth of domestic spending but greatly increased military spending in order to bring an end to the Cold War. After that, reduced defense spending helped President Clinton run budget surpluses from 1998 to 2001—the only period with a continuous surplus in the past 70 years.

The Bush administration increased social and military spending, reduced tax rates, financed a war by issuing debt, and added greatly to future spending for health care. Budget deficits and the gross debt rose and liability for future spending soared. The Obama administration greatly increased spending growth in 2009 and 2010. Gross debt reached $9 trillion, with additional unfunded promises of around $50 or $60 trillion. Foreign governments held about 25 percent of the debt, so much more of our future output must be used for exports to earn the money to pay the interest rate on the debt we owe. In 2009 the Obama administration proposed higher deficit spending to reduce unemployment and pollution, expand government-supported health care, and to redistribute income. The nonpartisan Congressional Budget Office (CBO) estimated that gross debt would nearly double in the next decade and said that without major policy changes, outstanding debt would reach 947 percent of GDP by 2084. Long before that point, a crisis would force policy change.

Reports of budget deficits and debt understate the government's future obligations. Estimates of the federal government's unfunded future liability for Medicare, Medicaid, and Social Security pensions range as high as $80 trillion, more than $250,000 for each currently living person. What this shows is that the political system makes promises that can't be kept—our political arrangements make it easier to promise benefits than to pay for them. Our country's choices are now restricted. Either we reduce spending to shift resource use toward more productive uses or we increase taxes to finance the welfare state. Welfare state spending helps the recipients, but it reduces national productivity, economic growth, and living standards.

The federal government is not alone. Many state and local governments have promised pensions to retired employees that can be honored only with much higher taxes. Or cities and states can renege on the promises, by making beneficiaries pay more of the cost. An alternative would shift the liability to the federal government, which is unlikely because the federal government has severe budget problems. Some estimates reach $2 or $3 trillion for these future state and local unfunded obligations.

Almost all state and local governments are required to balance their budgets annually. Instead of paying higher wages to teachers, police, firemen, and other employees, governments promised future pensions and health care that, being in the future, didn't affect the current budget but would come due only after the officials who made the promises were out of office. These obligations are now coming due. Few were fully funded in the interim. And states avoided the balanced budget requirement by employing schemes such as chartering government corporations that they excluded from the budget, exempting capital projects, and many others.

There is a tendency to make estimates of future costs that are overly precise and that later prove entirely wrong—mostly too low. The future is uncertain. By any measure, the costs of fulfilling the promises that have been made in the past are unsustainable. Something must be done to reduce future costs and develop a feasible, believable plan.

WHY THE CHANGE?

Over 50 years, the United States fiscal program went from prudence to profligacy. The change has four underlying causes: discretionary monetary policy; absence of a rule to restrain government spending; foreign aid and military commitments; and pressures for income redistribution.

Discretionary Monetary Policy

For most of the years from the founding to 1971, the United States was on a fixed exchange rate such as the gold standard or the Bretton Woods agreement. A country with large or recurring budget deficits lost gold and faced possible currency devaluation if gold reserves fell. Also, gold standard rules required participating countries to contract the money supply when gold flowed out of the country. Similar rules were part of the Bretton Woods agreement. Increasingly after 1965, the United States ignored the rules.

Such standards and rules were put into place to restrict a country's fiscal and monetary actions. For countries on the gold standard, inflation occurred in time of war, when governments usually suspended the standard. Restoring the pre-war exchange rate after the war required a country to accept deflation to restore the pre-war gold price. The United States followed this policy until the 1930s.

I have not favored a gold standard in the past, and I have not changed my opinion. The gold standard requires pro-cyclical monetary policy and willingness to accept as much unemployment as necessary to maintain the gold price. During economic expansions, gold flows into the expanding country, so monetary policy remains expansive while inflation rises. Then as gold flows elsewhere, monetary policy must contract, deepening the recession. Several economists noted this feature at the time. Also, the gold standard required countries to accept recessions to maintain the exchange rate. Citizens are no longer willing to pay this price. We no longer have the gold standard because the public does not prefer a fixed exchange rate to full employment.

President Franklin Roosevelt's governments ran budget deficits. During the 1932 campaign, Roosevelt sharply criticized President Hoover for his deficits and promised to balance the government budget, except for relief for the unemployed. His biographer, Arthur Schlesinger Jr., wrote that budget balance "was one of the few economic doctrines which Roosevelt held in a clear way—that an unbalanced budget was bad" (Schlesinger, 1960, 10). FDR maintained this principle by vetoing the 1936 pension payments to World War I troops, but Congress overrode the veto in an election year.

President Roosevelt finally accepted deficit spending in the 1938 recession. After six years, unemployment was still high in a Congressional election year. Several in the administration believed that New Deal policies had failed to restore growth and employment because they were too modest. Government spending and deficits increased after 1938, but growth did not return until the war.

After World War II, countries gave more prominence to domestic problems, especially unemployment. The Bretton Woods Agreement tried to reconcile domestic and international monetary actions by providing loans from countries with a current account surplus to countries with trade deficits. The idea, due principally to John Maynard Keynes, was that deficit countries could become more stable. Under the Bretton Woods system, countries with trade surpluses lent to countries with temporary payments deficits. Keynes believed that by borrowing, deficit countries would be encouraged to grow their way out of the debt and avoid contracting their employment and output.

The Bretton Woods system worked only for a short period. The United States dollar became the international currency. The United States and many other countries gave priority to maintaining domestic employment even if it brought higher inflation. Inflation in the United States spilled over to other countries, especially countries with a persistent current account surplus that did not permit their currency to appreciate enough to eliminate the surplus. They, too, yielded to political pressures to maintain employment and export growth. Deficit countries, especially the United States, would not devalue the dollar. Instead of a more stable system, Bretton Woods brought a sustained debate over whether deficit or surplus countries are responsible for adjusting.

By 1968, the United States restricted gold payments except to foreign central banks, and foreign central banks agreed to the restrictions. That brought the system near its end. In August 1971, President Nixon ended the gold exchange system by ending all gold payments.

The end of the Bretton Woods system recognized what had long been true. Countries, especially Great Britain and the United States, would favor their domestic concerns, particularly employment. An international agreement requiring stabilizing policies that went against these concerns would not be heeded and could not be enforced.

The end of Bretton Woods removed the last constraint on expansive policy. The United States took advantage of the international role of the dollar to finance budget deficits by expanding money growth. From 1980 to 2008, Asian countries, first Japan and later China, abetted this policy. China achieved sustained high economic growth through exports. To prevent its currency from appreciating, it imposed exchange controls at home and bought dollar securities at the central bank. This permitted the United States to maintain what President de Gaulle had called "an exorbitant privilege"—the right to pay for its deficits by borrowing in its own currency.

Vice President Cheney expressed the viewpoint of many politicians when he told Treasury Secretary Paul O'Neill that President Reagan had shown that budget deficits don't matter. He neglected to add, "as long as the Chinese (and others) buy the bonds to prevent a rise in interest rates."

The status quo will not be sustained, given the extraordinary budget deficits the United States is set to run from 2009 on. To restore stability, new rules for monetary policy must be set that will end excessive U.S. monetary and fiscal expansion and end Asian growth dependent on exports to the United States. These rules must be binding and enforced. In the next section, I propose a monetary rule.

A Commitment to Budget Balance

For more than a century, budget surpluses or balance was the American norm. The public opposed budget deficits, except in wartime. Under the influence of Keynes, and misreadings of him by later generations of economists, journalists, and politicians with a strong will to believe his prescriptions for the 1930s, the norm eroded. Deficits in recession could be viewed as a rigid policy prescription, which failed to comprehend Keynes's nuances or operating assumptions. By the 1950s the public accepted the principle of cyclically balanced budgets in which the government was expected to offset deficits in recessions by running postrecovery budget surpluses. The principle proved to be unworkable. Governments rarely could find the right time to end deficits.

After President Eisenhower, only the Clinton administration achieved a few balanced budgets. Democratic Congresses wanted to spend and redistribute income from upper income earners to others. Republicans, unhappy in the role of "tax collectors for the welfare state," failed to curtail welfare spending and abandoned their traditional call for fiscal responsibility. Seeing that liberal governments gained votes by increasing spending, they offered the same in reverse, attracting voters by offering tax reductions. By 1980, the U.S. Congress had two parties. One offered more spending, the other lower taxes and more spending. Deficits were criticized only by the party out of power. Democrats favored higher taxes on higher incomes. Republicans favored lower tax rates to promote investment and income growth. Neither party looked ahead to recognize that future deficits required future tax increases or reductions in spending.

From time to time, Congress would vote to require that additional spending or tax reduction had to leave the projected deficit unchanged—that is, be "budget neutral"—but this show of fiscal integrity had limited practical effect, as many loopholes and exceptions allowed Congress to circumvent the rules. The only successful effort to run a budget surplus after 1960 came in the last years of the Clinton presidency, with reductions in defense spending and a booming economy playing a large role.

For 20 years or more, analysts have pointed to massive future budget deficits in social security and government health programs. Congress has declined to discuss a solution. Future deficits in these programs are not on the current budget, so Congress ignores them, leaving the future crisis to a future Congress.

The solution to future budget deficits is obvious. Congress must reduce benefits in part by raising the age at which citizens can receive benefits, by increasing tax rates, or both. Neither is attractive to voters, so nothing happens.

Health programs raise the most difficult issues. Options include increasing efficiency of the delivery system in addition to reducing benefits and/or raising taxes. But there is no agreement on what is inefficient or what should be done. For example, almost everyone recognizes that to give tax benefits to employers for paying employee health insurance is inefficient, because it encourages waste and overspending. But because many of these benefits go to unionized workers, there is strong political support for maintaining the benefit.

Government rules setting payments for doctors favor specialists over family practitioners. One result is there are too few family practitioners. Another is that doctors order too many costly procedures. Further, a very large part of public spending on health care pays for services to patients in the last few months of life. Imposing copayments, graduated according to income, would not only reduce this spending but also shift medical services toward improved health care for the living.

To date the main solution has been to do nothing. Congress cannot agree on reducing benefits or increasing taxes, so by default agrees to push the problem into the future. Meanwhile, it adds new benefits without adding new sources of revenue.

Faced with the massive increases in spending and debt during the first two years of the Obama administration, the public voted for less spending and debt. In February 2011, 79 percent of the public agreed that the budget problem was "very serious." There was much less agreement about how much to reduce spending, which spending programs to cut, or who should bear higher tax rates. The age-old problem of who pays and who receives prevented consensus.

Many cities and states wrestle with a similar problem. Most cities and states are obliged to post balanced budgets each year (except for capital spending). In lieu of wage and salary increases, and in an effort to avoid increasing taxes, state and local governments promised union members pensions and other benefits chargeable to future budgets. To fund these promises fully would have increased current spending, so most were not funded, or not fully funded. As time passes, however, these future benefits become current obligations that either have to be paid by new taxes, abrogated by renegotiated contracts or new laws reversing the old, or defaulted on.

In Federalist 10, James Madison warned about the danger to democratic government posed by factions, which are the equivalent of today's special interest groups. In a political system that keeps most members of the legislatures and Congress in relatively safe seats, powerful interest groups block solutions. We are now facing the consequences.

To prevent budget deficits, Congress must adopt and follow a fiscal rule. The simplest rule would require a supermajority to have spending growth exceed growth of output except for wartime and deep recessions. In mild recession, the Congress would have to find a supermajority. Regulations should also be restricted to those which provide revenues to pay for mandates that shift costs to state and local governments or the private sector. An alternative would mandate cyclically balanced budgets, returning to the Eisenhower era policy but with strict enforcement of the rule by requiring mandatory reductions in spending once the economy recovers. Reducing the accumulated spending and debt will be difficult, but adopting and following a spending rule in the future will be harder still.

Foreign and Military Commitments

In the years just after World War II, the United States gradually accepted responsibility for maintaining world political stability and countering the perceived threat from the Soviet Union. This was one of the public goods provided as part of the postwar Pax Americana. This freed other countries to devote fewer resources to military spending and more to economic development and foreign trade.

The principal European countries contributed to defense but accepted U.S. leadership, as they could not defend themselves against possible attack by the Soviet Union. The end of the Cold War left them freer to pursue their own interests.

United States officials initially disclaimed the role of the world's policeman and tried to limit its role to defense against the Soviet Union and its satellites, but gradually, objectives broadened. At different times, the United States established bases in many countries, sending troops to defend Europe, Japan, Lebanon, Somalia, Dominica, Iraq, Vietnam, Korea, and Afghanistan, among others. Equipping military bases worldwide, maintaining a large navy to keep sea lanes open, protecting Middle East oil supplies on behalf of its allies in Europe and Japan, and providing a security umbrella for Israel, Saudi Arabia, Japan, Korea, Taiwan, and others, however, meant that the United States had taken on the policeman's role that it had sought to avoid—and with no rule or principle in place to restrict such involvements from widening and deepening.

Military experts rarely mentioned the costs of these operations. Neither the Johnson nor the second Bush administration included accurate cost estimates in their budgets. Presidents have used supplemental appropriations to keep military expenses out of the budget. Once a war is in progress, legislators find it difficult to vote against funding—so spending rises, mostly financed by issuing debt, which shifts costs from present to future taxpayers.

America received little support from its allies in most of its recent military expeditions, with a few exceptions, mainly Britain and Australia. (Canada has joined in Afghanistan.) Our major allies thus require the United States to bear most of the cost in blood, treasure, and effort. They are free riders.

The American public increasingly opposes protracted military efforts. In Korea, Vietnam, Iraq, and Afghanistan, the public initially supported the effort, but after a prolonged engagement with no victorious end or clear outcome, public support waned. The limits of America's responsibility urgently need discussion and clear decision making. Prominent citizens and the press will often urge the use of force to stop murder or persecution in places such as Somalia, Sudan, Rwanda, Kosovo, Iraq, or Libya, yet the United States has limited resources and cannot prevent all evils. We lack a coherent, credible set of principles to guide such decisions.

Congress controls the military budget, but as military bases and equipment contracts are spread across the country, members are reluctant to vote for reductions that threaten to hurt firms and families in their district. A few years ago, Congress agreed to let a commission choose which bases to close, reserving only the right to approve or reject the entire program. Although this arrangement got the job done, and bases closed, the weaknesses of democratic government were highlighted. Normal legislative processes had proved unable to make hard decisions.

Redistribution[2]

The federal government budget has also increased over the past 50 years as a result of efforts to redistribute income. Before 1960, Republicans and conservative Democrats favored balanced budgets. This was especially true of President Eisenhower. By the late 1970s, however, Republicans decided that they would never regain a majority in Congress merely playing the role of tax collectors for the welfare state. They became proponents of reducing taxes and simultaneously opposed spending restraints. Neither party slowed the growth of government-run welfare programs such as Medicare and Medicaid, thus ignoring countless warnings and demonstrations showing that the growth in federal spending for health care was unsustainable. Instead of slowing Medicare growth, in 2005 President Bush and Congress added on an expensive program to pay for prescription drugs, none of the additional costs for which were paid for by higher taxes. The Obama health care bill will also add substantial costs.

In many countries, taxes pay for government spending. Having run budget deficits over nearly all of the last 50 years makes the United States an outlier among developed countries.

In the absence of a widely accepted fiscal rule, such as a requirement that the peacetime budget stay in balance, politicians use expenditures and tax cuts as a means of attracting votes. A local Congressman or Senator will boast of securing federal funds for a local public works project, yet because most other elected officials are doing the same, the distribution of costs and benefits nationwide will differ. The net benefit to a citizen in one locality may be negative, after taking account of his or her share of the costs of projects undertaken in other parts of the nation.

In Pennsylvania, voters opposed the building of new football and baseball stadiums in public referenda by a large majority, but politicians found a way around the voters. By locating still more stadiums in other parts of the state with support from the federal government, the state legislature approved spending on stadiums in Philadelphia, Pittsburgh, and elsewhere. Despite their opposition, taxpayers were required to pay.

Outrageous examples are common. The "big dig" in Boston relocated roads and built a tunnel at a cost of billions to all taxpayers. This project mainly benefitted some local citizens. National subsidies go to some but not others. But all must pay.

Much political activity involves efforts to gain at the expense of others. Domestic politics very often answers the question: Who pays and who receives? In a modern developed democracy, most voters are in the middle class, so candidates for election or reelection offer programs to attract these voters. Older people benefit from publicly funded old age pensions and health care. Until recently few politicians supported changes that reduce benefits, despite clear evidence that they are unsustainably higher than future generations can be reasonably expected to pay.

Democrats usually favor higher taxes and more spending. They present themselves as the advocates of social justice and fairness, meaning income redistribution to the poor. Yet decades of their programs have done little to change the income distribution; the truth is that programs such as health and education direct spending mainly toward the middle class, where the voters are, not to the poor. Many retired people have modest current incomes, but they are not poor.

Republicans emphasize programs to increase economic growth by reducing tax rates, especially on the highest income groups. Broad-based income tax reduction lowered the highest marginal tax rate from above 90 percent in the early postwar years to a low of 28 percent in the 1980s, after Congress and the Reagan administration lowered rates and broadened the tax base by eliminating "loopholes" or special exemptions. Subsequently the highest marginal rate rose to 39.6 percent after 1992. State and local tax rates are an additional burden.

Promises to reduce marginal income tax rates have less appeal to the mass of voters now, because most income tax is now paid by people with income above the median. The income of the average voter is below the income of the median voter, so half the population has more than half of total income. The appeal of tax cuts depends on voters believing that tax cuts will stimulate the economy, causing middle-class incomes to grow, a less appealing proposition since the cuts of 2001 and 2003 did not do this. Growth rates rose, but middle-class income gains were limited by rising costs of health care and college education.

Voters hear the claims and counterclaims about fairness and growth, and they judge the outcomes. When years of government spending and higher taxes were followed by slow growth and rising inflation in the 1970s, enough voters complained about inflation that President Carter appointed Paul Volcker, a known anti-inflationist, to head the central bank. Volcker promised to reduce inflation. In the 1980 election, voters supported candidates who promised to raise economic growth and lower inflation. The British elected Margaret Thatcher and the United States elected Ronald Reagan on programs to lower inflation and increase living standards. Both succeeded, so voters continued to favor these policies. When growth slowed, followed by a serious recession, many voters wanted "change" and redistribution.

Pundits often forecast doom for the losing party after decisive elections that change the character of government. The prognostication is always wrong. The Johnson-Goldwater election, the Reagan-Carter election, and the Obama-McCain election produced much commentary of this kind, and the same occurs in other countries. Middle-class voters merely shift back and forth between choosing growth or redistribution.

Beginning in the 1970s, Congress adopted the earned income tax credit, which is paid to low-income workers as a way to induce them to choose work instead of welfare. Over time, the credit increased. In 2006, the lowest 40 percent of the income distribution received payments equal to 3.6 percent of tax revenues, and in recent years, the Obama administration has increased tax refunds to the lowest half of the income distribution. The top 5 percent pay about 50 percent of income tax collections. More than half of the people now pay little or no income tax. That means that tax reduction has lost much of its appeal as a political issue. Neither party proposes broad-based tax increases. Both, in office, proposed additional spending. President Bush's proposal to reduce future Social Security spending received support from neither party.

At some times, voters respond to the call for "fairness," and at other times, to "growth." This is true around the world. These shifts respond to the appeal of personalities, belief in the ability of candidates to do what they promise, and, perhaps most of all, to the perceived success or failure of the policies that are in place. Such swings in policy can continue until a rule limits the possibility of major fiscal change.

The evidence suggests that most redistribution programs benefit the middle class—the median voter in the model by Meltzer and Richard (1981). Although redistribution and "justice" wins at times and "growth" wins at others, the average tax rate in the United States does not change much. Sustained growth of output is relatively stable. When the growth rate falls, voters choose to raise it. When the income distribution changes, voters act to rebalance.

Efforts to redistribute income occur in many countries. They rarely change much. In many countries, the upper-income groups have increased their share of income for a decade or more. The principal reason is that returns to education dominate the change. Improved educational outcomes work to reverse the spread in income shares.

The United States especially has absorbed immigrants for more than a century. Discipline and self-discipline took some, often many, immigrants' children from poverty through educational attainment into the professions. Self-discipline in schooling and learning is now all too often absent for many who grow up in the inner cities. Learning requires effort by the student. More spending on education cannot correct for a lack of self-discipline or a determined parent.

CONCLUSION

Many countries with budget deficits finance their deficits with domestic savings. Japan is one big example. In Japan and some other countries, the deficits finance spending that brings little increase in productivity. Growth remains low. If voters do not choose a different path, the political-economic system sustains the low-growth equilibrium.

The United States has a much lower saving rate. Therefore, it finances its budget deficit by borrowing heavily abroad. The dollar serves as the world's main currency, and the United States has large, resilient asset markets. This international role of the dollar permitted the United States to finance budget deficits abroad for many years. One cost is that the dollar has depreciated against currencies with lower inflation and greater fiscal responsibility. For example, the Japanese yen and the Swiss franc are now one-fourth the exchange rate against the dollar that they were when the Bretton Woods system ended in 1971.

The only way to end continued deficits are higher tax rates, less spending, or both. Without a fiscal rule requiring responsible fiscal policy, budget deficits will continue until a crisis occurs. Much higher interest rates or a requirement that the United States sell debt denominated in foreign currency would indicate a crisis. Prudent policy would adjust the budget before a crisis. Prudent policy would start by adopting and following a budget rule that restored the old standard: a balanced budget or a surplus, except in wartime and deep recessions, and defining budget balance to account for the present value of future spending obligations and revenue.

The enlarged spending during and after the credit and housing crises that started in 2007 means that current and future deficits and outstanding public debt, and unfunded promises, are unsustainable. The test for democratic government will be to adopt a multiyear policy to restore stability without raising tax rates so high that investment and growth suffer. This will require reductions in military, defense, and nondefense spending at the expense of the promotion of income redistribution, "fairness," and "justice," through such spending. Some of the reduction can be done by raising the retirement age and the age for access to Medicare. A first step should be to emphasize spending, not deficits, because spending must be financed by present and future taxes. Deficits simply defer taxes or reductions in future taxes.

NOTES

1   Data are from Department of Commerce (1960, p. 711).
2   This section is based on earlier work with Scott Richard (Meltzer and Richard, 1981).

REFERENCES

Cecchetti, Stephen, M.S. Mohanty, and Fabrizio Sampolli. 2010. Working Paper. Basel: Bank for International Settlements, March.

Council of Economic Advisers. 2008. *Economic Report of the President*. Washington, DC: Government Printing Office.

Department of Commerce. 1960. *Historical Statistics of the United States, Colonial Times to 1957*. Washington, DC: Government Printing Office.

Meltzer, Allan, and Scott F. Richard. 1981. "A Rational Theory of the Size of Government." *Journal of Political Economy*, 89, 914–927.

Schlesinger, Jr., Arthur M. 1957–60. *The Age of Roosevelt*. Boston: Houghton Mifflin, 3.

4

SOURCES OF POSTWAR PROGRESS

THE HALF-CENTURY AFTER World War II is a remarkable period in world history. Living standards rose for more people in more countries than ever before. At the start, many predicted that the world economy would fall back into the low-growth and high-unemployment rates that had characterized the 1930s. Some believed the socialist states, the Soviet Union and its satellites, had the advantage, because they could plan resource use more efficiently.

The opposite happened—capitalist countries in North America, Europe, and Asia grew far more than the socialist states. Nikita Khrushchev's boast that "we will bury you" was, in essence, a claim that socialist planning was more efficient than capitalist freedom. By 1980, the competition was over. China and Vietnam accepted capitalist development, followed by India, which made the transition from socialist planning and direction to a more capitalistic system. By the end of the decade, the fall of the Soviet Union seemed to mark a definitive end to socialist planning.

Capitalism's edge was in putting many minds to work with the freedom to innovate, protected by the rule of law to protect personal and property rights, in place of a small group of planners. Competition between producers and sellers increases efficiency and reduces waste. And capitalism offers incentives to innovate in ways that add to consumer satisfaction. The Pax Americana, the postwar political and economic order that the United States initiated after World

War II, spurred development. The actions taken under Pax Americana were not always wise or well conceived, but they maintained political and economic stability and incentives for growth to a greater extent than in the interwar years.

After World War II, American power, inventiveness, creativity, and economic, military, and financial strength was unchallenged and in a class by itself. The United States proposed military and economic strategies to avoid war, contain the Soviet Union, and avoid any return to the destructive economic policies of the interwar years. The institutions that embodied and carried out these policies succeeded. They prevented a major war in Europe, ended the threat from the Soviet Union, and opened most of the world economy to trade. Prosperity was fostered, economic activity expanded, poverty declined, and there was greater economic and financial stability. More people in more places had higher living standards, better health, and more education, and they lived longer lives.

I call that period the years of the Pax Americana. It has now ended. The international institutions that sustained the successful policy still exist, but they no longer enjoy general acceptance. A large part of the U.S. electorate no longer supports the policy consensus that sustained the Pax Americana and contributed to its success.

Much has been written about international disagreements and reduced U.S. influence on international political decisions. Much of this commentary seems overstated. The United States remains strong militarily but divided about how to translate power into influence. And many critics at home and abroad want to require approval by the United Nations Security Council to use American military power. The principal international military alliance, the North

Atlantic Treaty Organization (NATO), was unable to adopt an effective response to a common problem in Afghanistan, Iran, North Korea, or Darfur. Today, many wonder why it or the United Nations should be permitted to constrain the world's principal military power. Developing a national consensus on the use of our power is much more relevant.

Economic changes are much less discussed but no less important, both domestically and internationally. There are two points. One is the weakening of international economic institutions. The other is domestic policy and politics.

At Bretton Woods and Havana, representatives of most of the world's market economies committed their governments to follow rules for trade and finance, led by the United States. The General Agreement on Tariffs and Trade (GATT), followed by the World Trade Organization (WTO), monitored trading practices and settled trade disputes. A series of agreements or "rounds" lowered remaining tariffs except in agriculture and many services.

Lower tariffs and trade barriers worked as expected. Many countries found their comparative advantage, opened their economies, and raised their incomes. The success stories in Asia especially are well known.

Japan took advantage of the new trading rules with an export strategy. By undervaluing its exchange rate and rigidly controlling capital exports, Japan expanded at annual rates of growth as high as 10 percent from the 1950s to the 1980s. By moving workers from agriculture to industry, maintaining quality education, and encouraging efficiency, Japan became the world's second largest economy. Productivity rose, but its most important component was the movement of laborers from agriculture to manufacturing. When that ended, growth slowed. But Japan also innovated in production by improving its production methods regularly. In time, it became the dominant producer of automobiles and many consumer durables.

After a destructive war in the early 1950s, South Korea followed policies similar to Japan's. It developed efficient steel and shipbuilding industries, invested heavily in education, and moved its economy toward industries with higher productivity. Korean students attend many U.S. colleges and universities.

Others joined the struggle for economic growth. Living standards rose dramatically in Hong Kong, Indonesia, Singapore, Thailand, Malaysia, and later Vietnam and China. Each of these countries adopted capitalist methods and encouraged foreign investment. Those (Vietnam and China) which had earlier attempted to use centralized planning as their development strategy wound up failing to provide sustained growth sufficient to lift many people out of poverty.

Near the end of the 20th century, India began to replace its version of socialism with the market-oriented strategy that its neighbors successfully used. The Indian growth rate rose from about 2 percent to 6 or 7 percent annually.

As Kant noted, humans are not perfect, and neither are the rules they design. Changing the rules to provide incentives for growth offered countries new opportunities. Under the GATT and WTO, countries were able to arrive at regional agreements that lowered costs, as did the European Union and the North American Free Trade Agreement (NAFTA). But NAFTA was opposed by organized labor and constituencies in the United States and Mexico. Despite much evidence of NAFTA's long-term benefits to the three signatories, politicians pander to the disaffected, who fear competition and favor protectionism. Instead of recognizing that the U.S. education system does not provide 21st-century job skills, they blame freer trade for the decline in real income experienced by those who are displaced. Kant's principle is at work here as elsewhere. Those who are injured do not choose to sacrifice for the common good.

The Doha (Qatar) negotiations show an inability to reach a compromise that would lower barriers to trade in agriculture in the developed countries and services in some of the principal developing countries. The United States (and others) turned to bilateral agreements, many of which have proved contentious. The high tide of multilateral trade agreements to reduce barriers to trade is probably past. Currently, the best future hope is that the United States and the European Union won't step up trade restrictions to compensate for foreign labor and environmental practices, as many critics earnestly advocate, and that China will stop subsidizing or giving other advantages to Chinese firms. Both seem a vain hope. Trade protectionists and nationalists everywhere seem eager to end the regime that brought sixty years of global expansion and rising living standards. This is a major change in the international landscape. It threatens a main source of higher living standards everywhere.

One of the oldest economic principles explains that reducing trade barriers benefits all parties to the agreement. It does not say that everyone in society gains. In all politics, those who lose are determined to make their grievances known, emphasizing the losses and neglecting the gains. Using misstatement and overstatement, they have been able to prevent new trade agreements.

The United States took the lead in promoting open trading arrangements and all countries that participated gained.

The negotiators that let China into the WTO neglected the need to condition that entry on China's adjusting its exchange rate, which China pegged to the U.S. dollar. By "managing" its exchange rates, China was able to promote low-cost exports. As in Japan during its high-growth years, exchange controls and credit controls limited the rise in prices for Chinese goods. That would have reduced their advantage. By 2010 China's resistance to exchange rate appreciation and large capital inflows increased inflation, depreciating the real exchange rate and raising the cost of goods produced in China. Many critics of China's policy do not recognize that the current Chinese inflation is an effective substitute for currency appreciation. Inflation and revaluation are equally effective ways of raising the real exchange rate and the cost of Chinese goods.

Export-led growth required a companion policy of import-led consumption or investment elsewhere. Policymakers in the United States recognized that U.S. consumers receive desirable goods and services in exchange for pieces of paper (money and bonds), produced at little cost. As always in trade arrangements, both countries gained. China reduced unemployment and poverty. It increased its output and improved its living standards and its global influence. The United States gained from low prices for consumer goods, but those who lost jobs for whatever reason complained that the trading system harmed the economy by ceding manufacturing to Asians.

The WTO system will survive in some form, but it will have a lesser role. Many in the United States and the European Union are willing, perhaps eager, to restrict imports—in which case, those who expect international trade to increase over the next 25 years at a pace similar to that of the past

SOURCES OF POSTWAR PROGRESS | **91**

25 years are likely to be disappointed. This will affect GDP growth rates in China, India, and other developing countries that depend on export-led growth. It is one among many reasons for doubting the more optimistic estimates of China's future growth, and for believing that world growth and economic progress will be weaker in a future marked by more protectionism.

The large amount of U.S. debt held by foreigners can only be serviced by increasing U.S. exports. The United States can no longer serve as importer of last resort for countries that practice export-led growth. This change requires adjustment at home and abroad.

The Bretton Woods agreement was part of an international effort to increase postwar stability, economic growth, and development by avoiding competitive devaluation. Between 1958 and 1971, the International Monetary Fund (IMF) worked to maintain fixed but adjustable nominal exchange rates. Britain and the United States negotiated the agreement and others signed on. The final plan was mainly a U.S. plan. The United States agreed to maintain the dollar price of gold at $35 an ounce. Other countries set their exchange rates in terms of the dollar or gold.

Soon after adopting Bretton Woods, Congress passed the Employment Act, committing the government to maintain "maximum employment and purchasing power." Neither term had a precise definition, but a 4 percent unemployment rate became a policy objective. No one recognized that the $35 gold price and the 4 percent unemployment rate would create a conflict. As inflation rose after 1964, gold outflow reduced the U.S. gold stock and threatened the fixed exchange rate system.

The system did not work as intended, and it did not survive. In practice, the United States maintained its unemployment objective, rather than policies consistent with its obligations under the Bretton Woods system. Inflation rose. In 1971 the United States embargoed gold sales, and in 1973 the Bretton Woods system ended de facto. When the system prevailed, the United States would not devalue the dollar against gold; other major countries were reluctant to revalue their currencies against the dollar. In 1971, the dollar, the British pound, and the Japanese yen adopted floating exchange rates. Most Western European countries also floated and later adopted a single currency, the euro. As in most modern fixed exchange rate systems, debtors wanted creditors to appreciate their exchange rates and creditors said debtors should adjust.

In the late 1990s, the IMF set out to recycle oil revenues, reform the former Soviet Union and its satellites, and do something about Asian countries that artificially pegged their currencies so as to distort trade between nations. Yet as financial markets grew, the IMF's role and influence declined. Most who borrowed from the IMF repaid their debt, thus reducing the IMF's income. From 2004 to 2007, IMF loans fell from US $102 billion to $15.82 billion in 2007. At that point, IMF had to cut back on its own budget, and it discussed selling gold to pay for expenditures. Several of its former clients had adopted stabilizing policies: Asian countries had accumulated about $4 billion in foreign exchange holdings to protect against sudden economic shocks. The Chiang-Mai initiative established a $120 billion fund to assist Asian countries if a crisis returned, in order to avoid recourse to IMF loans or crisis management. Even Turkey, one of the IMF's frequent borrowers, announced in the fall of 2009 that it preferred to manage without IMF support and interference. Throughout the world, the IMF was seen as a surrogate for policies that the United States espoused but didn't practice at home. Some argue it has devolved into a merely political organization. All studies of how IMF lends show that economic variables guide its lending, but a growing body of literature says that international politics is beginning to predominate.

The credit and housing crisis revived the IMF. At the London meeting in 2008, countries voted to increase IMF resources by US $500 billion, an increase agreed to in advance. Countries also voted to issue US $280 billion in new Special Drawing Rights (SDRs), which are a basket of international currencies that the IMF issues in proportion to recipients' GDP. As such, more than two-thirds of the additional SDRs will go to rich countries. Countries that are members of the IMF will also receive an allocation of SDRs, including Zimbabwe, Iran, Sudan, and Venezuela. These countries will exchange their SDRs for currencies they can spend.

Actual lending gives a different picture of IMF activity during the financial crisis. Between the end of 2007 and April 2010, the IMF increased loans outstanding by SDR 35 billion, about US $57 billion dollars at the then-current exchange rate. In 2009, the IMF issued SDR 280 billion, the full US dollar amount agreed to in London.

The new IMF made fewer demands on borrowers. Critics of its Asia policy in 1997–98 and new management changed the procedures. The IMF offered standby agreements for countries with conservative fiscal and monetary policy, as the congressionally appointed Meltzer Commission recommended in 2000 (Meltzer et al., 2000). Mexico was the first country to be granted the right to draw up to US $47 billion from the IMF to supplement its domestic reserves in a crisis.

The IMF lent to countries that had already borrowed and spent excessively, such as Ukraine, to whom it lent US $16.6 billion. Ukraine has an unstable government and a very divided electorate. After its last election, its new government boosted public sector wages and pensions by 20 percent. The IMF responded by reducing Ukraine's required holding of international reserves of capital. This was a mistake.

IMF also lent generously to still more countries with poor prospects, such as Hungary. Hungary's government spends 50 percent of GDP, primarily on debt service and current spending. The result? Hungary's budget remains in deficit and its economy continues to decline. Romania has a US $17 billion IMF loan, a projected budget deficit of 9 percent of GDP, and worsening economic prospects because of European turmoil. When the government announced spending cuts, such as a 25 percent reduction in public sector wages, it was met by strikes and demonstrations. In 2010, the IMF and the European Union made large loans to the Greek government. Greece's debt is unsustainable, so the additional loan from the IMF is unlikely to be paid in full.

The IMF also has a large (US $10.9 billion) loan to Pakistan outstanding, which is risky, given the inability of Pakistanis to form a strong, democratic government and the political instability in its western regions—but perhaps less so than the IMF's joint loan with the African Export-Import Bank of $800 million to Zimbabwe. The 2010 package of risky loans made to Greece contained some restrictions on government spending. Romania's government actually favored more reductions in spending than the IMF, which recommended higher spending on the poor and disadvantaged.

Many criticized the old IMF for its lack of concern about the impact of austerity programs on the poor. The new IMF worries a lot about income distribution. But is this compatible with achieving macroeconomic stability? More harm may come of high taxes for charity to the poor if it diverts funds for investments that might establish a basis for future prosperity.

What is more, the IMF's record of enforcing its fiscal and monetary rule on debtor nations is poor (Vreeland, 2006). Most governments tend to choose policies that their publics will accept. Stabilization policies seem to work best, provided they work relatively quickly. Long drawn out austerity programs are unlikely to succeed or remain in place.

The old IMF preached budget balance and fiscal restraint—urging countries to avoid currency devaluation by raising nominal and real interest rates. The new IMF does the opposite, endorsing government spending to help the poor. In the financial crisis, the IMF spent only a small part—$51 billion—of its greatly increased authorized resources.

The one thing about IMF that has not changed is its lack of ability to enforce the promises of reform that debtor nations make in exchange for their IMF loans (Vreeland, 2006). Internal research shows that most such promises are kept for only a year or less (IMF, 2003). Even knowing that, the IMF has not found any way to sanction countries in violation. At times, it has briefly withdrawn funding, but governments know from experience this is sure to be temporary.

The IMF's future role is limited, despite its recent infusion of funds. Higher international reserves in Asia and in Latin America free such nations from the need for IMF assistance. The early IMF was able to help countries with temporary trade deficits, but by the 1980s, international imbalances weren't temporary and weren't the result of trade deficits; most resulted from excessive borrowing in foreign currencies. When lenders did not renew loans, borrowers had to contract. IMF loans to the debtor country allowed the lenders to get their money back. The lenders received higher interest rates for taking foreign risk. The IMF bailed them out.

The IMF's more limited role means that the future will not be like the past. The Argentine default showed that the market works to resolve defaults, even when a large number of foreign creditors are involved. Argentina's was the largest default ever recorded. Bondholders were numerous and dispersed geographically. Agreement was achieved, and more than three-quarters of the bondholders accepted the terms. No public money or lending by international organizations was needed.

This change is desirable, I believe, but it also increases risk in international lending that private actors chary of being burned will react by reducing loans. Previously, many countries kept exchange rates fixed when lenders withdrew their loans. Often lenders received risk premiums to cover their risk of devaluation. By allowing lenders to withdraw at a fixed exchange rate, the country absorbed the losses, shifting these to its own taxpayers and wealth owners. Lenders were spared the losses they had been paid to take. The IMF lent reserves to help the country maintain its exchange rate, so the main burden fell on the citizens of the troubled country.

Hereafter, lenders will become more aware of the risks. All risks cannot be avoided. But countries can reduce risk by following stable policies. Instead of having policies dictated by IMF consensus reached in Washington, governments must adopt stabilizing policies that are in their interest, or else suffer the consequences. Those that do will get more private foreign capital at lower interest rates. Those that don't will get less investment and pay higher interest rates. It would be a change for the better. If lenders to countries that don't reform are made to accept the losses their risky lending entails, the new system will become more stable. The IMF's role will diminish.

The IMF's most valuable contribution will be to collect and distribute timely information about borrowing countries. Better information improves the operation of markets. The IMF should limit lending to countries that pursue prudent policies but are harmed by events in neighboring countries. Uruguay is an example of a country that suffered large capital withdrawals by Argentine depositors during the Argentine crisis at the start of this century. IMF loans enabled Uruguay to avoid a financial crisis.

Some see in the recent difficulties a reason for more rules and increased international regulation, but this view disregards the fact that a major cause of the crisis was the failure of national and international regulation. The Basel agreement required banks everywhere to adopt common standards, including a rule that required banks to increase their reserves as they increased their risk position. It never happened. Banks only shifted risk off their balance sheets so as to keep their capital levels low. New instruments distributed risk, but bank reserves did not increase, and distributing the risk did not eliminate it—it only globalized it. Instead of leaving the risk on the banks' balance sheets where regulators monitored transactions and holdings, the risk just became less transparent.

Failures of domestic regulation are common. The Securities and Exchange Commission did nothing to stop Bernard Madoff's fraud despite an informant who clearly demonstrated that he could not possibly be doing what he claimed. The Federal Reserve did its best to prevent the major U.S. banks from reporting losses on international debt in the 1980s. Although Chairman Greenspan warned about stock market "exuberance" in 1996, the Federal Reserve did nothing. And it failed again to act to mitigate the housing and credit market problems before 2007.

Recent experience illustrates yet again that lawyers will set rules and regulations, but markets will circumvent them without violating the law. The crisis in home finance is another example of this principle. Successful regulation is difficult because lawyers do not usually think about the economic incentives the regulation will create. Admittedly this is difficult to do. Markets devote considerable resources to circumvention, when it seems profitable to do so.

Regulation adopted hastily is usually bad regulation. The central problem in financial markets, I believe, is that policies that prevent failure—too big to fail—give traders an incentive to increase risk. How else to explain the purchase and sales of almost worthless securities by traders with MBA degrees from the world's best business schools? They failed to do the due diligence that should be expected. They were rewarded for these transactions, and often fired if they did not participate. The incentives have to change, not by regulation, but motivated by self-interest—fear of failure. Top management must have an incentive to say no to bad deals so as to avoid large losses at the end of the day. Regulators must renew the policies that make capitalism without failure akin to religion without sin. Capital requirements that make owners bear losses provide incentives for prudent behavior.

The United States no longer is able to develop plans that others will quietly accept. It retains an important role in the world, but it has less power and influence than in the past. Part of the change results from the success of America's postwar policies that encouraged many countries to develop. Part results from domestic political weakness, to which I now turn.

POLITICAL STALEMATE

Politics in the United States remains in a stalemate. Most observers recognize that health care, energy, and educational failures are old problems that government has not been able to solve. Yet government will not permit private solutions to apply when they can. Nearly continuous large budget deficits, enormous international debt, and crime continue. Congress has been unable to adopt solutions. Deficits in Social Security and Medicare are discussed endlessly without any action. Medicare's trustees estimate the present value of future Medicare net payments at $85 trillion, a figure reflecting a $10 trillion increase during the one year just before the 2010 health care legislation passed, which represents the unfunded liability created by the recent drug benefit entitlement program. Presidential candidates one-up each other with promises of more moons than their rival. Reforms end with yet more spending rather than reform. The health care debate epitomizes the absence of discipline in the political process to the extreme.

During part of the Reagan years, I served on PEPAB— the President's Economic Policy Advisory Board. We met a few times a year with the president to discuss his policies and counteract some of the opposition found in the press and parts of the bureaucracy. PEPAB reminded President Reagan to follow the principles to which he subscribed and not be deterred by opposition in the press and on television.

At one meeting, President Reagan announced that he favored a program to insure against catastrophic health care payments. Congress promptly approved a bill. The bill required all senior citizens to enroll and pay an insurance premium. That requirement recognized an insurance principle called adverse selection. A voluntary program would enroll mainly those who believed they were likely to develop a long-lasting, catastrophic illness. Others, who did not believe they would suffer, would not enroll. That situation would raise the cost of the program and put it beyond the reach of many. Hence, participation was mandatory.

The outcry was loud and sustained. Those who believed they wouldn't need it demanded repeal. Within a year, Congress repealed the program. It never went into effect.

The lesson I draw from that experience is that many more citizens desire better health care than are willing to pay for health care. A recent attempt to mandate comprehensive health care in California failed for this reason. The political process facilitates the belief that today's consumers can get the benefits by shifting the cost elsewhere.

"Elsewhere" turns out to be future generations. We have two political parties. One wants to spend more and tax the rich. The other is willing to spend more but wants to tax less. The usual compromise in recent decades is more spending but lower, or not higher, tax rates. The result in 2009 is an outstanding publicly held debt of about $4.5 trillion and rising, about half owned by foreigners and even larger—much larger—unfunded liabilities.

When Vice President Cheney told Treasury Secretary Paul O'Neill that Ronald Reagan showed that the deficit did not matter, he forgot to add "as long as foreigners finance most of it." It is true that $4.5 trillion is not an alarming percentage of GDP, but the percentage is now rising rapidly. Our children will be wealthier than we are, so they can manage to pay the cost of our health care and much else by servicing the debt we leave to them—or so we expect. We also leave a large capital stock and an extraordinary educational system at the graduate and research level.

The bigger problem is that we have put our country in a risky position. Current policy is unsustainable. We all know that unsustainable policies end. The problem is that we cannot know how they end. We can hope, against experience, that we will stop spending more than we produce and stop borrowing from abroad. The debt would level off or even decline. To complete that picture, we have to conjecture about why that will happen. We have rarely slowed domestic spending growth below income growth for very long. The Reagan and Clinton years are a main exception.

A benign outcome is not impossible but perhaps too much to expect, because the public's desire for increased spending and lower tax rates has not slowed. The alternative is that we will have a crisis of one kind or another. The dollar, which once traded at 360 yen and 4.25 Swiss francs, is now less than 100 yen and 1 Swiss franc. As long as the overall saving rate remains lower than investment, the declining trend is likely to continue. The political reaction is to blame foreigners for our current account deficits. The truth is that we save too little and spend too much relative to our income.

Almost 30 years ago, a government commission published *A Nation at Risk,* warning of the decline in the quality of education for large parts of our population. The government has not failed to introduce educational programs, but the problem remains and grows. We fail to train many of our children for 21st-century jobs. In our 50 largest cities, about half the children do not earn a high school diploma from a public high school. This restricts many of them to unskilled jobs. That affects our ability to compete in the world economy, threatens the global trading system, and increases demand for income redistribution.

Research shows that good family structure gives students the incentive to study and learn. A nation that educated millions of immigrants and their children over more than 100 years relied on parental discipline and self-discipline. In its place, some schools experiment with payments to students for mastering material. Monetary rewards increase incentives, and many students develop useful work habits.

The price of oil increased in 1973–74. In the more than 40 years that followed, seven presidents and many Congresses discussed the problem, talked loosely about energy independence, and changed little. For a time, they controlled the price, encouraging consumption. Businesses have responded by reducing energy consumption, and government has mandated increases in mileage per gallon for autos and trucks. However, President Obama thinks the solution is higher taxes on oil companies and large subsidies for wind and solar power that raise the user's cost of energy. A similar policy failed during the Carter years. Experience in Europe suggests that claims that our future lies with increased employment in the so-called green energy industries will not be realized.

The billions we pay to import oil goes to our adversaries. Because we are politically unable to agree on a policy to reduce oil imports, we furnish Saudi Arabia with the funds to build mosques that employ preachers who teach hatred of America. Iran can use the money we and others spend on oil to build nuclear weapons. Russia and Venezuela pursue hostile policies.

We arm in part to defend ourselves against these possible threats. If we had heavily taxed carbon 40 years ago, we would now pay ourselves instead of foreigners. We could not summon the self-discipline to do that, and our government did not call upon us to make the adjustment. Instead we pay others to induce us to consume less. Several use the money for unfriendly purposes.

A country that cannot solve its domestic problems does not inspire confidence. Inability to solve major problems hastens the end of the American century. To outsiders, our failure must be puzzling, since some of the problems have obvious solutions. A tax increase and benefit reduction phased in over time are certain to be a large part of any solution to budget deficits. Some type of carbon tax will be part of any program to reduce oil imports.

WHY NOW?

Through much of our history, the United States government maintained fiscal balance. Budget deficits rose during wars, but surpluses followed. Budget surpluses in every year from 1866 through 1893 paid down two-thirds of the government debt outstanding after the Civil War. By 1930, government surpluses had reduced by one-third the debt outstanding at the end of World War I. In the 1920s, Treasury Secretary Andrew Mellon reduced both tax rates and debt by running an annual budget surplus.

One can debate whether these were desirable policies. They were certainly quite different from current policy. Spending and tax policy remained disciplined except in wartime. This is no longer so.

Until World War II, or thereabouts, a majority of advanced nations accepted the international gold standard as the proper international system. I have never been an advocate of the gold standard because it requires acceptance, at times, of unemployment rates the public does not accept. We do not have the gold standard because we know its consequences for unemployment.

That said, the earlier belief in the gold standard protected the economy from continued large budget deficits. As long as the public supported that rule, governments could not run large, continuous, peacetime budget deficits. Along with the gold standard, the public accepted the logic and propriety of a balanced budget.

Continental countries have now adopted a single currency and thus a permanently fixed exchange rate. Although Italy and Belgium have large outstanding debts, the common currency maintained economic stability for a decade. By 2010, the absence of enforceable rules for prudent fiscal policy put the European system under considerable pressure. Efforts under way may lead to enforcement of budget policy on member states. The European response to the crisis shows the difficulty of achieving and maintaining stability. Despite a treaty commitment to avoid fiscal transfers to member countries, the European Union and the International Monetary Fund made large loans to Greece and Ireland. Instead of making bank stockholders and managers accept losses, the burden shifted to taxpayers, especially German taxpayers. In this, they followed the U.S. policy of protecting banks and bankers at taxpayer expense.

The United States currency is a world currency. Its debt has been the standard for safety of nominal values. Policies abroad favoring export-led growth and a domestic policy of import-led consumption permitted publicly foreign-held U.S. debt to grow without any noticeable effect on real interest rates. Real interest rates on U.S. debt didn't change much from the budget surplus years in the 1990s to the budget deficit years after 2001. Foreigners accumulated dollar denominated debt and financed our spending on their exports.

Once again, the solution is not difficult to see. Either the United States voluntarily adopts fiscal discipline or eventually it will face a crisis with rising interest rates and a falling currency. The crisis solution will impose large costs on holders of dollar-denominated debt, but it will force policy adjustment. If a voluntary solution is unlikely, the mystery is when the crisis will occur.

Voluntary solutions are rare until crisis forces change. Several countries in Asia faced fiscal and exchange rate crises in the 1990s. Korea and Indonesia made durable reforms. Crises forced political changes that in most cases were overdue. Argentina, Brazil, and Mexico suffered through several crises, with Brazil and Mexico making lasting reforms. The United Kingdom had repeated exchange rate crises from the 1950s to the 1980s that ended with fiscal tightening. The Thatcher government reforms put the country on a different path that successor governments kept up until recently.

Japan also has a large debt outstanding in absolute terms and relative to GDP. Quite unlike the United States, though, Japan has a relatively high saving rate. Domestic owners hold most of the debt. Debt-financed public projects reduce

Japan's productivity. Japan bore this cost internally. The risk to Japan, however, is much less than the risk to the United States because of its much higher saving rate. Japan's biggest problem is that too much of its saving is invested in government debt. The government uses the saving for large public projects that have low productivity, thereby lowering Japan's growth rate.

Political changes in the United States make voluntary change difficult. We are long past the Eisenhower era of fiscal responsibility when President Eisenhower could enlist the cooperation of the Senate majority leader Lyndon Johnson to prevent permanent tax rate reduction during the 1958 recession. The two parties have become less cooperative, indeed uncooperative, on major issues.

Once, the political parties were coalitions that resolved disputes internally. This is less true now. Campaign funding legislation weakened the parties by reducing their funding. Interest groups gained influence because they gained resources. Most of these groups had no interest in political compromise. They support candidates who commit to support their position, often an extreme position.

CONCLUSION

U.S. citizens have not agreed on a long-range program to solve its main problems. We do not have a shared vision of the way to maintain domestic and world growth. Leadership requires such a vision. A country that cannot agree on solutions to its domestic problems is an unlikely leader.

The future position of the United States is not entirely a negative tale. The United States has a more flexible economic system than most. It leads often in innovation and technological change. These are advantages in adapting to global changes.

An additional advantage is that there is no obvious leader that can replace the United States. As our influence and position wane, the world will be more dependent on willing cooperation by many countries. They must find means to agree on rules for trade, economic and political arrangements, and crisis management. This outcome is not likely to be more stable than the American Century. Nor is it as likely as the American Century to support institutions that benefit nations that choose peaceful economic development and higher living standards.

Rule-based policies for trade, finance, and political stability provided a framework that fostered exemplary growth in living standards for vast multitudes. The rules were not perfect. They were manmade, and so, subject to Kant's dictum. If we are to restore stability, countries must establish and enforce a new set of rules for trade, finance, and political stability that increase incentives for participants everywhere to cooperate, develop, and grow.

REFERENCES

IMF. 2003. *Fiscal Adjustment in IMF Supported Programs.* Washington, DC: International Monetary Fund.

Meltzer, Allan H., et al. 2000. *Report of the International Institution Advisory Commission.* Washington, DC: Government Printing Office.

Vreeland, J. R. 2006. "IMF Program Compliance: Aggregate Index Versus Policy Specific Research Strategies." *Review of International Organizations,* 1, 359–378.

5

FOREIGN AID

GOVERNMENTS OF DEVELOPED countries transferred more than $120 billion in overseas development assistance to less developed countries in 2008, with the United States contributing almost one-fourth of the total. As critics often point out, the per capita U.S. contribution ($530) was less than half that of citizens of Luxembourg and far below the 0.7 percent of GDP that nations promised to give. Only five countries reached the 0.7 percent goal.

Two reasons suggest that we should not be embarrassed by this. First, as the Hudson Institute (2010) has shown, private philanthropy from foundations, corporations, and others added $37 billion to government transfers. Second, the amount transferred is a poor measure of the benefits to the recipient countries. Kant's principle should warn us that larger financial transfers open possibilities for corruption, waste, bribery, and theft—which certainly abound in the history of foreign aid whose transfers seem to have done little for economic development.

Research by Easterly (2006), Moyo (2009), and Collier (2007) concludes that at best much development aid is wasted. Moyo argues that aid creates a culture of dependency that deters local action. Easterly suggests that the World Bank and others ignore simple but helpful projects, such as mosquito nets to prevent malaria, and spend on large-scale, wasteful projects that achieve little.

Haiti is an example of foreign aid that failed. As many as 3,000 nongovernment agencies provided goods and services after the 2009 earthquake. A year later, there are few signs of reconstruction or gainful economic activity. Most residents of Port au Prince, the capital, live in tents and depend on rations distributed by donors. The government is weak, corrupt, and ineffective. The institutional structure has not developed; the rule of law does not exist.

As Kant's principle warns, without the rule of law that gives incentives for honesty and fair dealing, crime will increase. Haiti is an unfortunate example of support by foreign aid without institutional structure and the rule of law. The history of aid failures can be extended at regrettable length.

In its 60-year history, the World Bank has tried several approaches to development, from offers of loans for programs the Bank wants (which are rarely successful) to ideas solicited and led locally, which economists came to realize were more likely to be successful.

In 1999, Congress appointed a Commission to study international agencies and recommend changes.[1] The Commission found that many of the Bank's loans were heavily subsidized—underwriting as much as 75 percent of the cost. Loans were commonly made for 40 years at a 1 or 2 percent interest rate with lengthy grace periods for repayment. Politicians in developing countries had, and were given, no incentive to direct scarce resources toward repayment. Consequently, many defaulted on the loans. Lending governments then voted to forgive the debts—building "moral hazard" that such loans could simply be considered free money that recipients would probably never need to repay.

The Commission recommended that the Bank recognize the level of subsidy in its loans and simply convert them into monitored grants, thus giving the Bank responsibility to monitor programs chosen by the recipient country. This allowed recipients to use the money as they rather than as the Bank preferred (IFIAC, 2000). The Commission said the Bank should implement "pay for performance," but monitoring, and then insisting on, performance has proved difficult for the Bank to implement, or the Bank has been reluctant or found it impossible to find ways to do so.

Research at the World Bank and its affiliates shows that performance on Bank projects has been mediocre. The Bank's self-evaluation for the 1990s gave it an overall 40 percent failure rate, concluding that corruption made it hard to prevent money from being diverted from projects into private accounts.

During the Cold War, loans and subsidies may have encouraged cooperation and assistance to the United States and its allies, although there is no systematic evidence of this. With the end of the Cold War, this argument loses force. Foreign aid does not today win the United States grateful friends. Egypt receives $2 billion a year from the United States but votes against U.S. proposals in the United Nations about 80 percent of the time. The United States went to war to free Kuwait from invasion by Iraq. Kuwait votes against U.S. proposals about two-thirds of the time. Most Arab countries, including the Emirates and Saudi Arabia, do the same. Democratic India and authoritarian Syria vote against U.S. proposals 80 percent of the time.

In 2008, the World Bank reported net overseas development assistance of $128.6 billion. This sum includes all disbursements on concessional terms net of repayments. Iraq, by far the largest recipient despite its instability, received $9.9 billion, 7.5 percent of the total. The 2008 loans were a substantial reduction from the $22 billion (20 percent of lending) in 2005. Notable also is the amount lent on concessional terms to Turkey ($2 billion), India ($2.1 billion), and China ($1.5 billion). Each of these countries has access to capital markets. Countries such as Sudan ($2.4 billion), Somalia ($758 million), and Pakistan ($1.5 billion) are highly unstable.

The lending data do not suggest that Bank administrators are giving careful consideration to how to promote growth, relax market constraints on funding, reduce corruption, or introduce incentives for growth. The World Bank is aware of the problems posed by corruption. "Corruption is the greatest obstacle . . . to reducing poverty," it says on its website. One paper on corruption in the construction industry notes that regulations are often ignored. It presents a chart showing a cross-section of incidence of corruption by industry, ranging from the most corrupt sectors, public works and defense, to the least corrupt, agriculture and fisheries (Kenny, 2010). There is little evidence that the World Bank has any effective policies against corruption. When President Paul Wolfowitz held up payments to countries with substantial corruption, the Bank's senior staff mounted a campaign against him and succeeded in bringing charges that forced him to resign.

The Bank has always been a lending institution. Staff is encouraged to make loans and is rewarded for doing so. Several studies of the Bank's performance reach this conclusion. So despite repeated criticism, the emphasis on loans rather than monitored grants continues (Sherman, 2010).

Other foreign aid agencies have many of the same difficulties of monitoring without linkage between promises and performance. Roger Bate studied the distribution of medicines provided by the Global Fund to Fight Aids, Tuber-culosis, and Malaria and found that "out of the 100 million high-quality antimalarial dosages donated approximately 30 million are diverted." About 20 percent are diverted by free clinic patients who sell the free drugs they obtain on the black market; 80 percent—or 24 million treatments—are resold directly from government storage and distribution facilities "with the support of local government officials, or at least without their interference" (Bate, 2010, p. 3). The program had no performance incentives. Payments were not made conditional on the number of successful inoculations or pro-gressive reductions in the incidence of disease. Such pro-grams would seem to assume that results can be willed into existence through good intentions. Kant knew better than to rely on universal benevolence. Institutional arrangements that schedule pay for performance may prove more effective than those that merely declare concern and good will.

Comparisons of countries with similar cultures after 40 years leaves little doubt that private market systems out-performed centrally planned economies. In 2010, North Koreans suffered from starvation and deprivation; South Koreans enjoyed a per capita income of about $20,000, and their economy continued to grow. Before its collapse, East Germans could see the greater wealth and prosperity of West Germany. And the remarkable growth spurt in Japan from the 1950s to the 1990s brought Japanese per capita income to 80 percent of the United States.

Japan developed a growth model that others in Asia later adopted. It opened its economy to trade, forcing producers to compete in world markets. It undervalued its exchange rate to encourage exports and restrict imports, and it con-trolled capital imports to prevent appreciation of its real exchange rate. Korea, Taiwan, and later China and Vietnam followed Japan's lead. Several adopted legal reforms to limit arbitrary actions by government and provide a framework of laws and institutions on which investors could rely. China has been slow to develop the rule of law.

Lerner (2009) compared growth in living standards in Jamaica and Singapore between 1965 and 2009. Both are small island economies. In 1965 per capita income was slightly higher in Jamaica: US $2,850 to US $2,650, using 2006 prices. By 2009, Singapore citizens had eight times the income of Jamaicans: $37,220 to $4,590.

Singapore grew six times faster than Jamaica over more than 40 years. Lerner explained the difference in growth rates as a result of better investment decisions, greater emphasis on education in Singapore, an absence of corruption, political stability in Singapore, and years of instability in Jamaica. He compared Singapore's stable, growing, market economy to Jamaica's inflation, socialism, instability, and complicated tax laws and regulations. Singapore enforced the rule of law.

Jamaica received US $128 million of grants in 2008. Singapore did not receive World Bank or U.S. aid. World Bank grants did not require Jamaica to adopt policies similar to Singapore's policy of maintaining rule of law and incentives for private investment.

Decades of research have not uncovered a formula for economic development that works everywhere. Singapore's rules and government interventions differ from Hong Kong's, but both are successful. Mexico opened its economy, adopted stabilizing macroeconomic policies, and reduced tariffs. Growth rates rose but not as much as in Chile or later Brazil or Peru. Nevertheless, it remains true that open economies that achieve macro stabilization and maintenance of the rule of law achieve much higher growth than socialist countries. No socialist country has achieved sustained development under socialist methods.

The World Bank makes frequent claims about its leading role in fostering development in poor countries. In 2010 45 percent of its outstanding loans went to five countries—Brazil, China, India, Mexico, and Turkey. Each of these countries could borrow in the capital markets. China, for example, is a large capital exporter that purchases claims and invests in raw materials in Africa and elsewhere. Why should these countries receive large, subsidized loans? Concessional loans from the World Bank and its affiliates should go to poor countries that adopt pro-growth policies, not to countries that can borrow in the capital markets.

The World Bank's Annual Report shows the stated purpose of its loans. Since money is fungible, the stated purpose may bear little relation to the use of the loan at the margin; so caution is needed when interpreting the data that follow. The Bank recognizes the important role of rule of law in economic development by having a lending category by that name. From 1990 to 2010, the Bank and IDA (its development subsidiary) made $353 and $169 billion total loans, respectively. It designated only 1 to 1.4 percent of the loans as loans to develop rule of law.

Properly organized and implemented foreign aid should principally serve humanitarian purposes. The World Bank has moved far from this goal, with much of its lending going to countries classified as "investment grade." Scarce funds should be reallocated from these countries to the poorest countries, where humanitarian aid reduces malnutrition and disease.

In 2000, the International Financial Institution Advisory Commission made recommendations to restructure Bank lending (IFIAC, 2000, p. 86):

1. The Bank should allocate most of its funding to relief of destitution in the poorest countries.
2. The Bank should phase out lending to countries that reach investment grade.
3. The Bank should recognize that its resources are a small part of the financial resources that the developed countries transfer to the developing world.
4. Monitored grants should replace loans for economic development.
5. Bank programs should more actively endorse programs to expand the rule of law, free markets, and open economies.

Too many good intentions will be wasted unless performance incentives are included in Bank lending programs. The current program of monitored grants gives too little attention to monitoring and incentives. Grant payments should be tied to measures of performance such as the number of children vaccinated, the number of students capable of reading, the number of houses receiving clean water. Monitoring should be certified by independent agencies, so as to eliminate any incentive on the part of the lending agency to "cover-up" any emerging evidence of program failures. Reduced corruption would be an important side benefit of more focused monitoring.

Poverty reduction is too important to be left to the chance that political officials will behave in enough of a hands-on way to make programs work. Kant's message implies that

monitored incentives are required to produce desired outcomes. Grants monitored by independent agencies might
encourage performance by ensuring that payments are
reduced or eliminated when countries do not achieve
objectives.

The World Bank is a development agency that should not
involve itself with programs that don't contribute to development and poverty reduction. During the presidency of James
Wolfensohn, the Bank initiated many programs to change
social arrangements in client countries. Instead, resources
should have been directed toward the Bank's main objectives—
improved living standards.

In June 2010, the *Wall Street Journal* reported that
Afghan officials left the country with suitcases filled with aid
money from the United States Agency for International
Development, an extreme example of a problem prevalent in
many countries. Corruption in Afghanistan reaches high
levels of government, which can hardly be incentivized to
reduce corruption through improved program design, inas-
much as they are its source.

Some environmental programs penalize poor countries
severely. Laws requiring corn-based ethanol in gasoline
raises food prices everywhere, especially in countries that
use corn meal as a dietary staple. The United States is the
world's largest corn producer. Currently 40 percent of the
corn crop is turned into automobile fuel at greatly increased
corn prices. Environmental activists promoted the program
politically with assistance from farmers. Politicians ignored
those who warned that ethanol would not reduce air pollution, and, to boot, would consume more energy in production than using gasoline alone. The evidence shows that these
warnings were correct. Yet ethanol subsidies not only remain

in effect, they have increased, for its corn subsidies remain popular with farmers.

Ethanol is only one example. The Danish statistician Bjorn Lomburg has given many other examples of costly programs that accomplish little. Estimates suggest that European governments' climate policy will reduce growth by $250 billion a year for the next century but reduce temperature very little. Eager environmentalists cite the British government's Stern report despite its flawed analysis: it does not discount future benefits, so its estimates of benefits in the distant future are overvalued.

CONCLUSION

Foreign aid to impoverished people has been a stated objective of officials in developed countries for many decades. Large sums transferred to governments have achieved much less in terms of relief of poverty and destitution than market opening, rule-of-law, and market freedom.

Government-to-government programs exemplified by the World Bank and its affiliates and privately funded aid programs face similar problems of corruption and lack of commitment by recipient governments.

In the 60 years following World War II, more people in more countries have had living standards raised and poverty reduced than in any previous epoch. The force driving change was institutional change, often a shift from a planned economy to a market economy. Korea, China, India, Poland, the Baltic states, Chile, and Brazil are leading examples. There are many differences between countries, and some have been more successful than others. The differences are important, and the reasons for them are not well understood. The main lesson, however, is that incentives change as institutions change. As Kant taught centuries ago, corruption and malfeasance are properties of individuals that institutions mute or amplify. The more concentrated the power, the more likely is corruption. Capitalism disperses power and limits corruption.

NOTES

1   I served as chair of the Commission.

REFERENCES

Bate, Roger. 2010. "Do Aid Agencies Want to Know When Their Medicines Go Missing?" *Health Policy Outlook*, 5, Washington, DC: American Enterprise Institute, December.

Collier, Paul. 2007. *The Bottom Billion: Why the Poorest Countries are Failing and What Can be Done About It.* New York: Oxford University Press.

Easterly, William. 2006. *The White Man's Burden: Why the West's Efforts to Aid the Rest Have Done So Much Ill and So Little Good.* New York: Penguin.

Hudson Institute. 2010. *Index of Global Philanthropy and Remittance.* Washington, DC: Hudson Institute.

IFIAC. 2000. *Report of the International Financial Institution Advisory Commission.* Washington, DC: Government Printing Office.

Kenny, Charles. 2010. "Construction, Corruption and Developing Countries." World Bank website, WPS 4271, December.

Lerner, Josh. 2009. "Jamaica vs. Singapore." *The American,* November 19. [http://www.american.com/archive/2009/november/jamaica-vs-singapore].

Moyo, Dombisa. 2009. *Dead Aid.* New York: Farrar, Straus, and Giroux.

Sherman, David. 2010. http://www.WorldBankUnveiled.com.

6

WHY INFLATION WILL RETURN

THROUGH MOST OF our history, inflation occurred during wars. Until the 1930s, peacetime federal government spending rarely exceeded 3 percent of total spending, so there was little pressure to finance government by issuing money. Budgets usually had a surplus. Large wartime spending was financed by deficits, borrowing, and money growth. Wartime inflation followed, but when peace returned, so did budget surpluses. Typically, countries suspended the gold standard during wars, restoring it after wars ended. This severely restricted peacetime inflation.

The gold standard served as a rule limiting money growth and interest rates. If money growth rose too much, the gold stock fell. Policymakers had an obligation to maintain the gold price by reducing money growth and raising interest rates. This slowed the economy and increased unemployment. When gold flowed in, money growth rose, and the economy expanded until inflation rose.

Low average inflation, even price stability, are the well-known benefits of the gold standard rules. The disadvantages were that it required countries to accept unemployment and lost output in order to stabilize gold flows at a fixed gold price. As many economists pointed out at the time, a related disadvantage was that the gold standard was backward looking because it responded with a lag to past gold flows. That reinforced business cycle fluctuations.

We no longer have the gold standard, because democratic governments, reflecting voters' concerns, prefer now to keep unemployment rates low rather than stabilize prices via the price of gold.

The high point of the international gold standard was 1870 to 1913, when most trading countries complied with that system, suspending compliance during World War I. The United States formally joined the system in 1900 but had informally followed gold standard rules for many years before. The United States did not suspend the rules during the war.

In December 1913, Congress approved and President Wilson signed the Federal Reserve Act establishing a central bank to manage money, smooth interest rates, and respond to cyclical changes. The United States was on the gold standard, so the Federal Reserve had only limited discretionary authority to change interest rates and money.

After the First World War, leading central bankers in Europe and the United States worked to restore a weaker version of the classical gold standard. The Great Depression ended these efforts—deflation was now the Federal Reserve's main concern, not inflation or the exchange rate. Over time, countries directed their efforts to reducing unemployment. In 1946, Congress approved the Employment Act, directing economic policy to maintain maximum employment and purchasing power. In practice this imprecise goal became "full employment," which for many years meant a 4 percent unemployment rate.

The Federal Reserve controls a short-term interest rate and provides for increases in bank credit and money by buying government debt. The more it buys, the faster the growth of money and credit. Inflation occurs when money growth persistently exceeds output growth. Maintaining money growth slower than output growth first reduces output growth, followed by declining inflation or even falling prices. Proper monetary policy seeks to steer between these two extremes in the effort to achieve steady growth and low inflation or price stability. Achieving these objectives, however, is rare for the Fed.

In principle, the Federal Reserve is independent of politics. Federal Reserve officials often say they are independent *within* government, not independent *of* government. In practice, in the 1960s and 1970s, that often meant that the Fed helped the government finance its frequently large budget deficit by buying some of the government's bonds and issuing money. This undermines central bank independence in its role of holding down interest rates, for when the Fed buys the government's debt, it encourages budget deficits, money growth, and inflation.

Once the gold standard ended, the Federal Reserve had much more freedom to decide what interest rate and money growth it would provide. It used that discretion badly. The Fed's record is poor: it includes the Great Depression of the 1930s; the Great Inflation of the 1970s; several recessions and business cycles; and, most recently, keeping interest rates low too long, which contributed to the financial crisis by encouraging buyers to take out mortgages to buy houses. Unlimited discretion allowed the Federal Reserve to bail out large banks and other companies during the recent crisis, thereby shifting the losses from bad loans onto the taxpayers.

Housing policy, not Federal Reserve policy, and a lapse in what most of the market assumed to be effective regulatory oversight but later turned out to be large-scale fraudulent debt packaging for securitization and sale to others, is the main cause of the recent financial crisis. There were many private sector and government errors leading up to the crisis, but the crisis would not have occurred if mortgages had not been offered to people who made no down payment, had no equity invested in their house, and had poor credit histories or even none at all. Government housing policies that urged banks to lend to bad credit risks also invited defaults. When housing prices started to fall, mortgage defaults soared. A large percentage of the low-quality mortgages are owned by government agencies, so taxpayers will bear billions of dollars in losses. Housing policy and the subsequent debacle is another in the long history of well-intentioned programs that ended in disaster. In this instance, the desirable end was to spread home ownership to people without access to mortgage credit.

MONETARY POLICY IN THE POSTWAR YEARS[1]

President Truman is the only president to pay for a war mainly by raising tax rates. His successor, President Eisenhower, was a fiscal conservative who proposed balanced budgets and even surpluses, except during the deep 1957–58 recession. With small government debt issues, the Federal Reserve could usually keep money growth low, so inflation and interest rates remained low. At the end of the Eisenhower presidency, inflation had been eliminated. The public expected it would remain low in the future, as in other peacetime years.

Critics faulted the Eisenhower policies. They pointed to recessions in 1954, 1957–58, and 1960 and compared slower U.S. growth to growth abroad, especially in Germany and

Japan. They blamed conservative Eisenhower budget policy and accompanying monetary policy for the problems they saw. Candidate Kennedy ran for president on a program to "get the economy moving." In office, he later proposed to reduce tax rates for businesses and households and to deliberately run a budget deficit.

After President Kennedy's assassination, President Lyndon Johnson persuaded Congress to enact the tax cuts that Kennedy had proposed. The Johnson administration leaned hard on the Federal Reserve to help finance the budget deficit by holding interest rates low and letting money growth increase. At the time, the Federal Reserve believed it was independent "within" the government (rather than "from" the government), and did what was asked. The Fed shared the belief that its first responsibility was to keep the unemployment rate at around 4 percent. At the time, many economists and policymakers believed they could trade off higher inflation to obtain lower unemployment. In his presidential address to the American Economic Association, Professor Milton Friedman pointed out that any reduction in unemployment would be temporary if it were brought about by increasing inflation.

Economic growth rose after the tax cuts. The public liked increased growth and increased employment at rising wages. The policy was an economic and political success. Popular views about budget deficits shifted to a belief that deliberate decisions to run budget deficits could bring prosperity. Public support for conservative budget policy diminished. By the late 1960s, the money growth rate remained consistently above the real growth rate. The Great Inflation was under way.

Richard Nixon won the 1968 election. He promised to reduce inflation without causing a recession. His advisers told him that no one knew how to do that, but he persisted. Looking ahead to the next election, President Nixon told his advisers that no one ever lost an election because of inflation but, he said, recalling his experience in the 1960 election, they did lose if unemployment rose.

President Nixon appointed his friend and adviser, Arthur Burns, as Federal Reserve chairman. Burns was a distinguished economics professor who had served as Chairman of the Council of Economic Advisers during President Eisenhower's first term. Burns had warned Nixon in 1960 about the coming recession. Nixon considered that recession the main reason he lost that close election.

In 1971–72, all the members of the Federal Reserve Board except Chairman Burns had been appointed by Presidents Kennedy and Johnson, and they had no interest in aiding President Nixon's reelection. Their main concern was unemployment and the slow recovery from the previous recession. Chairman Burns, however, was eager to help the president gain reelection; privately, President Nixon often pressed Burns to increase money growth to help him get reelected. The Nixon administration adopted "temporary" price and wage controls to defer any price pressures and to shift most economic stimulus toward employment. Burns and the other Federal Reserve Board members agreed that more stimulus was desirable, even necessary, to reduce the unemployment rate, and Burns was a leading advocate of price and wage policies. Key members of Congress who were responsible for supervising the Federal Reserve actively supported the expansive policy.

Once he was reelected, the president gradually removed price and wage controls. Reported inflation soared, helped along by the first large increase in oil prices. The Federal

Reserve slowed money growth. Members told each other about their commitment to bring inflation down, and probably meant it at the time.

The commitment didn't last. The first effect of slower money growth fell on output and employment. When the unemployment rate rose above 7 percent, the commitment to reduce inflation vanished. More monetary stimulus induced more spending, followed by still higher inflation. Throughout the 1970s, the Federal Reserve repeated this sequence. Their staff predicted inflation from its estimated Phillips curve, which predicted that lower inflation would cause unemployment to rise. Since they wanted to reduce unemployment, they remained willing to have more inflation, even though they agreed it wouldn't increase employment permanently. They planned to reduce inflation later.

Throughout the years of rising inflation the Federal Reserve concentrated on near-term outcomes. The staff forecast longer-term consequences, but board members mostly focused on what they could do about current unemployment, never discussing the long-term consequences of their actions.

Staff forecasts of inflation persistently underestimated the inflation rate. Aware of the error, members nevertheless didn't correct it. And, contradicting the Phillips curve model of inflation and unemployment on which the staff relied, inflation and unemployment rose on average through the decade. Increases in money growth, and expectations that inflation would continue, became the main inflationary force.

After a second surge in oil prices, reported rates of inflation reached double digits. Daily news reports told about rising gold prices. Inflation talk was ever-present. For the first time, public opinion polls reported that by a large margin the public regarded inflation as the main domestic problem. That soon brought change.

President Carter hadn't earlier expressed much interest in reducing inflation, but he now faced reelection. Public concerns became his concern. Administration economists weren't much help. They offered new proposals that the president urge restraint on labor unions and large corporations. The president knew previous efforts to "jawbone" had failed. He turned to a known anti-inflationist, Paul Volcker, appointing him to head the Federal Reserve. Volcker told the president he would reduce inflation. The president assured him that was what he wanted.

Volcker had great experience for the job. Most of all he had commitment. Within two months of his appointment, he completely changed the Federal Reserve's operations to concentrate on reducing inflation. He knew it would take time, so he reduced concentration on short-term changes in employment and interest rates. He let the market set interest rates. The Federal Reserve worked to control money growth.

Volcker knew his policy would raise the unemployment rate initially. Asked on a Sunday talk show if he would have to abandon his efforts when unemployment increased, he explained that he did not plan to repeat this familiar pattern. Inflation and unemployment had increased together over time. He expected them to decline together. Abandoning the Phillips curve, he put in its place a very different idea: the best way to get lower unemployment was to have low inflation. Though he praised the Federal Reserve staff, he also forthrightly told them that their forecasts of inflation based on the Phillips curve were unreliable.

Most investors remained skeptical. They had heard Federal Reserve officials announce anti-inflation policy several times before, each time only to abandon the effort after unemployment rose. Interest rates continued to rise. Long-term Treasury bonds reached 15 percent, the highest interest rate ever.

Volcker persisted. In May 1981, with the unemployment rate at 8 percent and rising, he let the short-term interest increase—a startling difference from the past. Short-term interest rates rose to an astonishing 20 percent. Volcker later admitted that this was far above anything he anticipated. He continued on.

Markets saw that Volcker intended to succeed where others had failed. By the summer of 1982, both inflation and short-term interest rates fell. The inflation problem was on its way to being solved, but Volcker's problems were far from over. Lower inflation caused the dollar to appreciate. Foreign governments, especially in Latin America, had large debts denominated in dollars. The cost of servicing and repaying the debt soared. And high long-term interest rates made new government borrowing very expensive. Starting with Mexico, foreign debtors began to default. At home, Volcker faced similar problems. Several banks and other mortgage lenders faced bankruptcy because the rates they paid to borrow remained above the rates they received on long-term mortgages. Housing starts tumbled. Many farmers borrowed to buy more land during the 1970s, expecting food prices to continue rising. When inflation slowed, many were unable to service their debts. Home builders faced severe distress. The unemployment rate headed toward its peak, 10.8 percent, the highest since the Great Depression and higher than the worst of the 2007–09 recession. Volcker began gradually to reduce short-term interest rates. He warned his colleagues about the many possible disasters that might occur, but was much less candid with the public. Although the Federal Reserve began to lower interest rates in July 1982, he didn't announce the policy change until October, at which time he suggested the change was temporary.

Markets responded strongly to the end of austerity. Recovery began, aided by lower inflation and the Reagan administration's tax cuts. But markets were skeptical about longer-term prospects. Interest rates on Treasury bonds remained above 10 percent until 1985, almost three years after short-term rates fell to a more traditional range. The recovery occurred despite real long-term interest rates as high as 7 percent a year.

Recovery without renewed inflation restored confidence that the Federal Reserve and President Reagan remained committed to low inflation. The next 17 years, 1985 to 2002, are the best period in Federal Reserve history. Inflation remained low, output growth relatively stable. Recessions remained mild. Economists call this period the Great Moderation. The Clinton administration followed stable tax and spending policies and ran budget surpluses several times. Monetary policy differed from other periods, also. The Federal Reserve came close to following a policy rule proposed by John Taylor.[2]

In 2003, the Federal Reserve, convinced that prices would fall, lowered interest rates so as to avoid deflation and allow credit to expand. These actions helped finance the housing boom, followed by a housing bust of dramatic size. Government policy encouraged banks and government agencies that financed mortgages to lend to borrowers who made no down payment and had no credit record. That policy invited increased defaults. When housing prices started to fall in 2007, the housing crisis was under way.

In the 1970s, the Federal Reserve prevented the failure of First Pennsylvania Bank because they believed it was "too big to fail." Although the term was never defined precisely, it seemed to mean that this bank's failure would weaken other banks and lenders from whom First Pennsylvania had borrowed. To avoid this risk, the Federal Reserve lent to First Pennsylvania, thereby preventing its failure. The bailout encouraged the belief, known as moral hazard, that large banks could take more risk because the government would always bail them out. And they did. Many banks increased their size to get into the government safety net. When the financial crisis came, policymakers again used taxpayer money to prevent banks, other financial institutions, and even automobile companies from declaring bankruptcy.

I have often said: "capitalism without failure is like religion without sin." It does not work well because it removes the dynamic process that makes stockholders responsible for losses and disciplines managers who make mistakes. Citigroup, a large New York bank, has been rescued several times. Managers learned very little about avoiding risk. "Too big to fail" gives political authorities the power to choose when to prevent failure and when to allow it. Capitalism works best when it is subject to the rule of law. Choosing firms that are too big to fail substitutes the rule of man for the rule of law. Unlike Citigroup, Drexel Burnham Lambert was allowed to fail, but public authorities arranged the rescue of Long Term Capital Management. Arbitrary, yes. Violation of the rule of law, yes. Invitation to corruption and favoritism, yes.

Arbitrary decision making by public officials creates uncertainty that adds to the crisis atmosphere during periods of economic stress. A terrible example in 2008 nearly wrecked the world financial system. In March, the Treasury, the New York Federal Reserve Bank, and the Board of Governors agreed to rescue a financial broker-dealer, Bear Stearns, by assuming some of the bad debts and selling the firm to the JP Morgan Chase bank. Market participants, especially those with large losses on their balance sheet, sighed in relief. They thought things would be back to business as usual—rescue the failures and shift some of the losses to the taxpayers. Some industry leaders expressed their relief publicly.

In October, the rules changed without warning. Lehman Brothers was not saved. Soon after, markets panicked. Uncertainty reigned. Financial institutions everywhere rushed to hold cash and avoided transacting. Chairman Bernanke and Treasury Secretary Paulson made the terrible mistake of changing the rules suddenly in the midst of a deep recession. To his credit, Chairman Bernanke did his best to prevent the panic from spreading. The Federal Reserve greatly expanded its lending and developed creative ways of helping many different institutions. It returned to its former policy of "too big to fail," by lending large sums to a failing insurance company, AIG. After a few weeks, the panic subsided. By March 2009, the first signs of expected recovery appeared in the markets.

The Federal Reserve increased its consolidated balance sheet from about $800 billion to more than $2 trillion. Most of the new loans had a short term to maturity. The Federal Reserve said that, as the loans reached maturity, its balance sheet would shrink, thus avoiding any large expansion of money and credit. Chairman Bernanke explained that his intention was to let the loans decline as they reached maturity. But that was not what he did. As the short-term loans came due, he violated two well-established central bank rules.

First, he replaced the expiring credits with long-term mortgages and securities backed by mortgages. Well-run central banks maintain very liquid portfolios consisting mainly of short-term assets such as 90-day U.S. Treasury bills. Second, he did the Treasury's fiscal job for it, by supporting the mortgage market. At the Treasury's public urging, he committed to buying $1 trillion of these securities to help stabilize the mortgage market. Well-run central banks don't get involved in credit allocation and fiscal operations. Adopting discretionary policies for short-term advantage risks inflation.

Chairman Bernanke announced that as the mortgages reached maturity, he would let them decline, which would start to shrink the amount of excess reserves sitting idle in the banks. Again, that didn't happen. When the mortgages started reaching maturity, he replaced them by buying long-term government bonds, leaving the amount of excess reserves above $1 trillion, an unprecedented volume. He then changed policy by further increasing excess reserves by almost $600 billion.

In a sluggish economy with slow growth and little demand to borrow, the risk of inflation remains low. As the economy recovers and borrowing increases, these excess reserves will support a large, inflationary increase in money growth. Instead of acting to reduce excess reserves, Chairman Bernanke encouraged his colleagues to increase them. His reasoning shows the continued focus on very short-run changes. Output growth is often highly variable from quarter to quarter. Slowing growth during the 2010 summer had people in brokerage firms predicting a new downturn, which didn't happen. By fall, economic growth shifted up. If the Federal Reserve had waited, I believe it would have avoided the mistake of a very large, additional increase in reserves.

Currently, in speeches and Congressional testimony, Chairman Bernanke repeats his commitment to price stability. But, he adds, fulfilling the commitment by raising the short-term rate above 0.25 percent must wait until the unemployment rate comes down considerably. As long as unemployment remains at 8 or 9 percent or higher, he assures the public that inflation is unlikely.

His argument relies on the Phillips curve, the same argument that led the Federal Reserve astray in the 1970s. The grain of truth in his argument is that it is more difficult to raise prices when demand is sluggish. But there are many reasons to be skeptical that this is the whole story. Price expectations shift around enough to make any simple relation between inflation and unemployment unreliable, as Chairmen Volcker and Greenspan often told the Fed staff. They brought inflation down and kept it low by ignoring predictions from the Phillips curve.

In Spain, the current unemployment rate is above 20 percent and rising. The Phillips curve would predict falling prices, but that isn't happening. In Britain, unemployment and inflation have increased in the past year, inconsistent with the Phillips curve but consistent with U.S experience in the 1970s and 1980s when inflation and unemployment moved together instead of in opposite directions.

As we enter 2011, the United States has large, unsustainable budget deficits and rising debt. Governments usually pressure central banks to keep interest rates low to hold down the cost of financing deficits, as occurred in the 1930s and 1940s and again in the 1960s and 1970s in the United States. Unprecedented excess reserves permit inflationary increases in money. The falling exchange rate suggests that traders expect the dollar to continue to depreciate. And it already

has, even against relatively weak currencies beset with difficulties, such as the euro and the Japanese yen. Large budget
deficits, huge excess banking reserves, and a depreciating currency are the raw materials of inflation. The Federal Reserve
does not have a credible plan to prevent rising inflation. Paying interest on reserves, it suggests, will get banks to hold
more reserves. Certainly true, but that still leaves more than
$1 trillion of excess reserves, which are inflationary.

Congress gave the Federal Reserve a dual mandate: keep
both inflation and unemployment low. It is inefficient and
costly to shift from one goal to the other and to ignore the
long-term effects of actions geared to the short term. The best
period in the nearly 100-year history of the Federal Reserve
was from 1985 to about 2002, when the United States experienced relatively stable growth and low inflation. During
those years, the Federal Reserve more or less followed a Taylor rule, responding to both objectives of the dual mandate.

After the financial crisis, the Federal Reserve's unprecedented $1 trillion increase in commercial bank reserves to
expand money and bank credit must be reduced if a new
round of inflation is to be prevented. This requires gradually
increasing the short-term interest rate while maintaining
rates low enough to encourage economic expansion and
increased employment. The Taylor rule offers a means of
carrying out the dual mandate.

POLICY FOR THE FUTURE

For countries that adopted it, the classical gold standard had
two benefits—low average inflation rates and stable exchange
rates. Countries abandoned the gold standard because it

sacrificed employment to maintain the price of gold and the exchange rate. Any serious effort to restore the classical system must be multilateral. A single country that restored the gold standard would buffer shocks from all parts of the world; that would be unstable and costly. There is no interest in restoring any type of gold standard in other countries.

I propose an alternative that would give some countries stable exchange rates and price stability without restoring the gold standard. The major currencies—the dollar, the euro, and the Japanese yen—should commit to maintain a common inflation rate and a fluctuating exchange rate, say 0 to 2 percent inflation. China could become a fourth member, provided that it allows its exchange rate to fluctuate freely and accepts the common inflation rate. Any country that wished to import low inflation could fix its currency to one or more of the major currencies. Countries that adopted that policy would recover the benefits they lost when the Bretton Woods system ended in 1973, and they would import the low inflation rate adopted by the principal countries. For their part, the United States, members of the European Central Bank, and Japan would have low inflation and a fixed exchange rate with countries that chose to participate. Many will point out that this system is not ideal. They are right. It is better than what we have had; it is voluntary; and it is a way of achieving the objectives of low inflation and more stable exchange rates.

Fluctuating exchange rates for major currencies permit the real (inflation adjusted) exchange rate to adjust to differences in productivity growth in major countries, thereby leaving these countries some ability to respond to changes in unemployment rates.

Participation in the proposed system would be voluntary. The only requirement would be the 0 to 2 percent inflation rate. As under the gold standard, markets would judge whether countries were maintaining their commitment to low inflation. No international meetings to coordinate policies would be needed. Decades of unrestricted discretionary policy have not brought many years with low inflation and stable growth. To improve on its record, Federal Reserve actions should be restricted by a rule. The Federal Reserve now has great authority but it is not accountable to the public. When it makes large errors, the public can hold only its elected political leaders accountable. The Fed should adopt and announce a rule announcing what output and inflation combination they intend to seek over the next two or three years. If the Fed fails to achieve its targets, it should offer an explanation along with the resignations of the responsible officials. Unanticipated events often cause policies to miss their objectives. The president can either accept the explanations of Federal Reserve officials, or their resignations. This would give the Federal Reserve ample incentive to achieve its targets and align accountability with responsibility.

This is not whistling in the dark. In the 1980s I proposed this arrangement on a visit to New Zealand's Reserve Bank. They improved the policy by negotiating an inflation target with members of the government. Following its introduction in New Zealand, 20 or more countries adopted similar policies.

FINANCIAL REGULATION

In many countries, the central bank is responsible for the supervision and regulation of commercial banks and other financial institutions. Some countries separate monetary policy and bank regulation by establishing a regulatory agency separate from the central bank.

Neither arrangement works very well for two main reasons: capture and circumvention. Capture occurs when the regulating agency appoints regulators who are too close to the industry it is regulating. The Securities and Exchange Commission (SEC) is an agency often said to be captured by the financial firms it regulates. Lawyers who have served at regulated firms, and so tend to favor the industry's point of view (which may or may not be the correct point of view from the perspective of the objective public interest), are chosen for regulatory jobs at the SEC, and young lawyers join the SEC before moving on to higher paying jobs in financial firms. Recently the SEC failed to prevent or pursue the Ponzi scheme that Bernard Madoff used to rob his investors of $50 billion, even after having been tipped off on its details by knowledgeable outsiders. Madoff's was a large fraud but by no means the only example of regulatory failure and capture.

The first in my three laws of regulatory circumvention is that markets learn quickly how to circumvent new regulations that the lawyers and bureaucrats in regulatory agencies impose. Regulations that are costly to comply with and to administer make circumvention easier. There are many examples. As interest rates rose in the 1960s and 1970s, commercial banks found themselves having to pay depositors rates dictated by regulation that fell below market rates. Banks tried to circumvent this regulation through schemes such as compounding interest, giving gifts, and offering free parking, followed eventually by regulators outlawing many of the circumventions. Depositors found new ways to bank so as to get market rather than submarket rates for their money, such as banking in London banks or buying money market funds instead. In the 1980s, the regulators ended interest rate regulation to enable commercial banks to compete with less restricted foreign banks and the money markets.

The second law of regulation says that regulations are static whereas markets are dynamic. As the cost of regulation increases, regulated firms and others devote resources to finding ways of getting around regulation, as with interest on bank deposits undermined by mutual funds. After a crisis in the commercial paper market in 1970, the Federal Reserve deregulated bank certificates of deposits of $1 million or more so that they would pay market interest rates. Some nonbanks, mainly mutual funds but also stock exchange brokers, bought the large certificates and offered to sell shares to smaller depositors. Depositors withdrew funds from banks to invest in the new money market funds, circumventing government caps on interest payable on commercial bank deposits.

My third law of regulation says that regulation is most effective when it changes the incentives of the regulated. Various laws, such as patent and copyright law and their associated regulations, grant monopoly rights to individuals who then defend their monopoly positions.

After the financial problems following the Enron scandals, Congress hastily passed the Sarbanes-Oxley bill in response to media criticism about a rotten core in American companies. There were a few rotten companies, headed by dishonest leaders; as Kant taught us, people are imperfect. Among the many companies, we must expect a few dishonest people.

Many warned that Sarbanes-Oxley would stifle companies from going public by increasing the costs of public listing. This proved true: the number of new stock issues declined after passage. The new rules discouraged managers from taking the public company route to expansion—this meant that new companies were made to suffer for the regulators' failure to spot fraud and dishonesty in time to protect the public.

During the 1980s, regulators failed also to protect the public. Many thrift institutions that served as the mainstay of the home mortgage market faced bankruptcy. Regulators eased accounting standards and in other ways worked to hide impending failures. This certainly didn't help the building problems; it probably made them much worse. Many of the thrift institutions failed, leaving behind a $150 billion loss for taxpayers.

At about the same time, many large banks faced large losses on loans to foreign countries, mainly Latin American countries, after Mexico's default in 1982. The Federal Reserve worked with the International Monetary Fund to increase lending to the debtor countries and use the new loans to pay the interest on the debt. Banks weren't required to recognize their losses; rather, debtor countries that couldn't service their existing debts were pushed deeper into debt. This process continued for more than five years. It ended when the large banks, not the regulators, finally recognized their losses by writing down the value of the debt. In 1989, a new administration developed a successful way of reducing the amount that countries owed. But the delay proved extremely costly to the indebted countries.

These failures of regulation had no effect on policymakers when faced with a new crisis. In 2010, Congress responded to the recent financial crisis by enacting hundreds of new regulations, the Dodd-Frank bill. Most of the regulations in the bill bore no relation to the problems in the financial system that had caused the massive losses. One of the worst was the requirement that the Federal Reserve regulate consumer credit through a regulator independent of the Federal Reserve Chairman but empowered to use the Federal Reserve's earnings for purposes chosen by the regulator.

The Federal Reserve earns its income by holding government debt. The 12 regional Reserve banks hold the debt, but the newly appointed consumer credit regulator can use these earnings without approval by either the Reserve banks or by Congress. This violates the rule of law and the spirit of the Constitution because the U.S. Constitution authorizes Congress to decide on spending and budgets, not unaccountable agencies. One cause of the recent crisis was the purchase of risky mortgages by government-chartered housing finance agencies (and the proliferation of this process by the private sector). Adding a new unsupervised off-budget agency is a major mistake.

Since the mid-1970s, regulators have treated large financial institutions as too big to fail. "Too big to fail" transfers losses from bankers to taxpayers and reduces some bankers' incentives to be prudent. The problem generally occurs when the secretary of the treasury has to make a decision about whether to let an insolvent bank fail and its stockholders bear the losses after any remaining valuable assets are purchased by another bank or shift those losses to the taxpayers. Many of his staff will tell him that allowing the bank to fail will run the risk of triggering a panic and a financial crisis, and "this crisis will go down in the history book with your name on it." I have found it impossible to counter this argument in a way that is convincing. It is not enough to tell the secretary to take the risk in the long-term interest of taxpayers and the rule of law or to explain the risks of moral hazard.

Dodd-Frank put the secretary of the treasury in charge of a committee to determine when to invoke "too big to fail." This is certain to be ineffective, since most secretaries of the treasury choose to bail out large banks. The new law makes two major errors.

First, the most effective way to end bailouts is to require banks to hold more capital. Banks that are protected against failure can borrow at lower interest rates than other banks. Instead of this implicit advantage, banks should be required to increase the proportion of capital they hold relative to assets as asset size increases. The largest banks would then hold the most capital relative to assets. Mistakes would be borne by owners and managers. Owners would have an incentive to monitor risks, and managers would have greater incentive to lend prudently. Incentives would replace prohibitions that exhort good behavior.

The staffs of regulatory agencies are currently busy writing new rules, and they are besieged by lobbyists and bankers seeking to circumvent the regulations by writing in loopholes. Some will succeed. Instead of this active scramble for control of the financial system, Congress should scrap the Dodd-Frank bill and replace it with the incentive of making stockholders and managers bear the burden of loss.

There were many bank failures in the 1920s, and even more after the start of the Great Depression in the 1930s. Most were small banks. Few large banks failed until late in the horrendous downturn. Major banks held capital equal to 15 to 20 percent of their assets. Last year world central bankers meeting in Switzerland agreed to increase capital for all banks. The next step should be to graduate the capital requirement by size of bank.

Taxpayers and voters can get better regulation and lower their costs by making the owners of firms bear the cost of their mistakes. They should insist on this. Kant's principle warns against the good intentions of officials. The only thing that can be relied upon are clear, simple rules that limit official discretion.

Capitalism works best in a stable environment that permits people to achieve their plans. To achieve the growth and freedom that only capitalism provides, countries must adopt rules that force policymakers to plan for the medium term and prevent inflation.

NOTES

1   This section is based on Meltzer (2009).
2   Taylor (1993).

REFERENCES

Meltzer, Allan H. 2009. *A History of the Federal Reserve: Volume 2, 1970–1986*. Chicago: University of Chicago Press.
Taylor, John B. 1993. "Discretion versus Policy Rules in Practice." *Carnegie-Rochester Conference Series on Public Policy*, 39 (December), 195–214.

INDEX